AI for Data Science

ARTIFICIAL INTELLIGENCE
FRAMEWORKS AND FUNCTIONALITY
FOR DEEP LEARNING, OPTIMIZATION, AND BEYOND

Zacharias Voulgaris, PhD
Yunus Emrah Bulut

Technics Publications
BASKING RIDGE, NEW JERSEY

2 Lindsley Road
Basking Ridge, NJ 07920 USA
https://www.TechnicsPub.com

Cover design by Lorena Molinari

Edited by Sadie Hoberman and Lauren McCafferty

First Edition

First Printing 2018

Copyright © 2018 Yunus Emrah Bulut and Zacharias Voulgaris, PhD

ISBN, print ed.	9781634624091
ISBN, Kindle ed.	9781634624107
ISBN, PDF ed.	9781634624121

Library of Congress Control Number: 2018951809

Contents

Introduction

There is no doubt that *Artificial Intelligence* (commonly abbreviated *AI*) is making waves these days, perhaps more than the world anticipated as recently as the mid-2010s. Back then, AI was an esoteric topic that was too math-heavy to attract the average computer scientist, but now, it seems to be a household term. While it was once considered sci-fi lingo, it's now common to see and hear the term "AI" featured in ads about consumer products like smart phones.

This is to be expected, though; once an idea or technology reaches critical mass, it naturally becomes more acceptable to a wider audience, even if just on the application level. This level refers to what AI can do for us, by facilitating certain processes, or automating others. However, all this often gives rise to a series of misunderstandings. As AI itself has become more well-known, so have spread various ominous predictions about potential dangers of AI — predictions that are fueled by fear and fantasy, rather than fact.

Just like every other new technology, AI demands to be discussed with a sense of responsibility and ethical stature. An AI practitioner, especially one geared more towards the practical aspects of the field, understands the technology and its limitations, as well as the possible issues it has, which is why he talks about it without hyperbole and with projections of measured scope – that is, he projects realistic applications of AI, without talking about scenarios that resemble sci-fi films. After all, the main issues stemming for the misuse of a technology like this have more to do with the people using it, rather than the technology itself. If an AI system is programmed well, its risks are mitigated, and its outcomes are predictably positive.

About AI

But what exactly is AI? For starters, it's nothing like what sci-fi books and films make it out to be. Modern AI technology helps to facilitate various processes in a more automatic and autonomous way, with little to no supervision from a human user. AI initiatives are realistic and purely functional. Although we can dream about what AI may evolve into someday, as AI practitioners, we focus on what we know and what we are certain about, rather than what could exist in a few decades.

AI comprises a set of *algorithms* that make use of information – mainly in the form of data – to make decisions and carry out tasks, much like a human would. Of course, the emulation of human intelligence is not an easy task; as such, the AIs of today are rudimentary and specialized. Despite their shortcomings, though, these modern systems can be particularly good at the tasks they undertake, even better than humans. For example, an *AI system*, which is a standalone program implementing one or more AI algorithms, that is created for identifying words from speech, can be more accurate than humans doing the same task.

It's important to note that all the AI systems we have today possess what is termed *narrow artificial intelligence*. This means that current AIs can do a limited set of tasks (or even just a single task) quite well, but offer at best mediocre performance at any other task. For instance, an AI might be great at figuring out your age based on a headshot, but that same AI almost certainly couldn't tell a classical music piece from a pop song.

Some AIs are designed to be used in robots, such as those designed for rescue missions, able to navigate various terrains. Other AIs are specialized in crunching data and facilitating various *data analytics* tasks. There are even AIs that emulate creative processes, like the AIs that generate artistic works, using the patterns they deduce from catalogs of existing work. *Chatbots* and other such

AIs are focused solely on interacting with humans. The possibility of a more generalist AI (called *Artificial General Intelligence*, or *AGI*) exists, but it may take a while before it can manifest, or before we are ready to integrate it into our world.

Since all this may sound a bit abstract, let's clarify it a bit. If a system can make some decisions by capturing and analyzing signals related to the problem, that's an AI (sometimes termed "an AI system"). You've probably used an AI, even if you didn't know it. Online radios like Spotify and Pandora use AI to recommend songs, and virtual assistants (like Siri) use AI to help you troubleshoot. Factors that help us decide whether a system is AI include the system's sophistication, its versatility, and how able it is to perform complex tasks.

Professor Alan Turing was the first to talk about this topic in a scientific manner. Upon studying this subject from both a theoretical and a practical perspective (through the creation of the first modern-day computer, used to crack the Enigma code in World War II[1]), he envisioned machines that could think and reason much like humans.

One of Professor Turing's most famous thought experiments is now named after him. The Turing test is a simple yet powerful *heuristic* for determining if a computer is advanced enough to manifest intelligence. This test involves taking either a human or a computer, and concealing it with another human. Another human, known as the examiner, then asks each of them a series of questions, without knowing which is which. If the examiner cannot determine from the answers to these questions whether he is speaking with a human or a computer, then the computer is said to have passed the test. This simple test has remained

---

[1] https://bit.ly/2mEHUpc.

a standard for AI, still adding value to related research in the field in various ways.[2]

AI facilitates data science

So, how does AI fit within *data science?* After all, folks have been working in data science for years without these fancy AI algorithms. While it is certainly possible to gain valuable insights using traditional data science, AI-based algorithms can often bring about better performance in our *models* – the mathematical abstractions we create to simulate the phenomena we study. In highly competitive industries, this extra performance gained from AI-based *data models* can offer an edge over others in the market. Because many companies in these industries already have abundant data they can use to train the AI algorithms, we term them *AI-ready*.

AI is now far easier to apply than ever before. The early developers of AI have proven that AI can deliver a lot of value to the world, without the help of a rocket scientist to make it work. This is largely thanks to a series of powerful AI *frameworks* and *libraries* that make AI methods more accessible to most data science practitioners.

In addition, AI has now diversified and matured enough to outperform conventional data science methods in many applications. For this, we must thank the increased computing resources at our disposal, particularly computing power. This is something made possible due to the *graphics processing units (GPUs)* becoming cheaper and easier to integrate to a computer, as add-ons. What's more, *cloud computing* has become more mainstream, enabling more people to have access to a virtual *computer cluster*, which they customize and

---

[2] https://stanford.io/2useY7T.

rent, to run their AI projects. This makes AI systems easily scalable and cost-effective, while at the same time fostering experimentation and new use cases for this technology.

All this cooperation between AI and data science has led to a lot of research interest in AI. Research centers, individual researchers, and the R&D departments of various large companies have been investigating new ways to make these AI algorithms more scalable and more robust. This naturally boosts the field's impact on the world and makes it a more attractive technology—not just for the researchers, but for anyone willing to tinker with it, including many entrepreneurs in this field.

So yes, data science *could* continue to happen without AI. But in many cases, this wouldn't make much sense. It is now clear that the world of data science has a lot of problems and limitations that AI can help address. The overlap of these two closely related fields will only continue to grow as they both develop, so now is the perfect time to jump into learning AI with both feet.

About the book

This book covers various frameworks, focusing on the most promising ones, while also considering different AI algorithms that go beyond *deep learning*. Hopefully, this book will give you a more holistic understanding of the field of AI, arming you with a wide variety of tools (not just the ones currently in the limelight). With multiple tools at your disposal, you can make your own decision about which one is best for any given data-related problem. After all, a good data scientist must not only know how to use each and every tool in the toolbox, but which tool is right for the job at hand.

Although most technologists and executives involved in data-driven processes can benefit significantly from this book, it is most suitable for data science professionals, AI practitioners, and those in related disciplines (such as *Python* or *Julia* programmers).

A basic understanding of data science is an important prerequisite to this book (for a thorough introduction to this, feel free to check out the book "Data Science Mindset, Methodologies, and Misconceptions" by Technics Publications). Moreover, a good mathematical background is recommended for those who want to dig deeper into the methods we examine in this book. Ultimately, though, the most important qualifications are determination and a curious nature, since you will ultimately put this knowledge into practice building your own AI systems.

Although this book is heavy on programming, you can still derive some useful understanding of AI, even if you don't do any coding. However, for best results, we recommend you work through the various examples and perhaps experiment a little on your own. We created a *Docker* image of all the code and data used in the book's examples, so you can follow along and experiment. See Appendix F for how to set up this environment and use the corresponding code.

This book provides an easy transition for someone with some understanding of the more well-known aspects of AI. As such, we start with an overview of the deep learning frameworks (chapter 1), followed by a brief description of the other AI frameworks, focusing on *optimization* algorithms and *fuzzy logic* systems (chapter 2). The objective of these first two chapters is to provide you with some frame of reference, before proceeding to the more hands-on and specialized aspects.

Namely, in chapter 3 we examine the MXNet framework for deep learning and how it works on Python. The focus here is on the most basic (and most widely used) deep learning systems, namely *feed forward neural networks* (also known as *multi-layer perceptrons*, or *MLPs* for short). The two chapters that follow examine these deep learning systems using other popular frameworks: *Tensorflow* and *Keras*. All of the deep learning chapters contain some examples (provided as Jupyter notebooks with Python code in the Docker image) for hands-on practice on these systems.

Chapters 6 through 8 examine optimization algorithms, particularly the more advanced ones. Each chapter focuses on a particular framework of these algorithms, including *particle swarm optimization (PSO)*, *genetic algorithms (GAs)*, and *simulated annealing (SA)*. We also consider applications of these algorithms, and how they can be of use in data science projects. The programming language we'll be using for these chapters is Julia (version 1.0), for performance reasons.[3]

After that, we look at more advanced AI methods as well as alternative AI systems. In chapter 9, specifically, we examine *convolutional neural networks (CNNs)* and *recurrent neural networks (RNNs)*, which are quite popular systems in the deep learning family. In chapter 10, we review *optimization ensembles*, which are not often discussed, but merit attention in this era of easy parallelization. Next, in chapter 11, we describe alternative AI frameworks for data science, such as *extreme learning machines (ELMs)* and *capsule networks (CapsNets)* which are either too new or too advanced for the mainstream of the AI field.

In the final chapter of the book, we mention about big data, data science specializations, and to help you practice we provide some sources of public datasets. The book concludes with some words of advice along with resources for additional learning. For example, in Appendix A we'll talk about *Transfer Learning*, while the topic of *Reinforcement Learning* will be covered in Appendix B. Autoencoder Systems will be briefly described in Appendix C, while *Generative Adversarial Networks (GANs)* will be introduced in Appendix D. Appendix E will take a look at the business aspect of AI in data science projects, while for those new to the Docker software, we have Appendix F.

---

[3] For a brief tutorial on the language, you can watch this YouTube video: http://bit.ly/2Me0bsC.

This book contains a variety of technical terms, which are described in the glossary section that follows these chapters. Note that the first time a glossary term appears in the text of the book, it is marked in italics. The glossary also includes a few terms that are not mentioned in the text but are relevant.

The field of AI is vast. With this book, you can obtain a solid understanding of the field and hopefully some inspiration to explore it further as it evolves. So, let's get right to it, shall we?

## CHAPTER 1

Deep Learning Frameworks

Deep learning is arguably the most popular aspect of AI, especially when it comes to data science (DS) applications. But what exactly are deep learning frameworks, and how are they related to other terms often used in AI and data science?

In this context, "framework" refers to a set of tools and processes for developing a certain system, testing it, and ultimately deploying it. Most AI systems today are created using frameworks. When a developer downloads and installs a framework on his computer, it is usually accompanied by a *library*. This library (or package, as it is often termed in high-level languages) will be compiled in the programming languages supported by the AI framework. The library acts like a proxy to the framework, making its various processes available through a series of functions and classes in the programming language used. This way, you can do everything the framework enables you to do, without leaving the programming environment where you have the rest of your scripts and data. So, for all practical purposes, that library is the framework, even if the framework can manifest in other programming languages too. This way, a framework supported by both Python and Julia can be accessed through either one of these languages, making the language you use a matter of preference. Since enabling a framework to function in a different language is a challenging task for the creators of the framework, oftentimes the options they provide for the languages compatible with that framework are rather limited.

But what is a *system*, exactly? In a nutshell, a system is a standalone program or script designed to accomplish a certain task or set of tasks. In a data science setting, a system often corresponds to a data model. However, systems can include features beyond just models, such as an I/O process or a data transformation process.

The term *model* involves a mathematical abstraction used to represent a real-world situation in a simpler, more workable manner. Models in DS are optimized through a process called *training*, and validated through a process called *testing*, before they are deployed.

Another term that often appears alongside these terms is *methodology*, which refers to a set of methods and the theory behind those methods, for solving a particular type of problem in a certain field. Different methodologies are often geared towards different applications/objectives.

It's easy to see why frameworks are celebrities of sorts in the AI world. They help make the modeling aspect of the *pipeline* faster, and they make the *data engineering* demanded by deep learning models significantly easier. This makes AI frameworks great for companies that cannot afford a whole team of data scientists, or prefer to empower and develop the data scientists they already have.

These systems are fairly simple, but not quite "plug and play." In this chapter we'll explore the utility behind deep learning models, their key characteristics, how they are used, their main applications, and the methodologies they support.

About deep learning systems

Deep Learning (DL) is a subset of AI that is used for *predictive analytics,* using an AI system called an *Artificial Neural Network (ANN).* Predictive analytics is a group of data science methodologies that are related to the prediction of certain variables. This includes various techniques such as classification, regression, etc. As for an ANN, it is a clever abstraction of the human brain, at a much smaller scale. ANNs manage to approximate every function (mapping) that has been tried on them, making them ideal for any data analytics related task. In data science, ANNs are categorized as machine learning methodologies.

The main drawback DL systems have is that they are "black boxes." It is exceedingly difficult – practically unfeasible – to figure out exactly how their predictions happen, as the data flux in them is extremely complicated.

Deep Learning generally involves large ANNs that are often specialized for specific tasks. Convolutional Neural Networks (CNNs) ANNs, for instance, are better for processing images, video, and audio data streams. However, all DL systems share a similar structure. This involves elementary modules called *neurons* organized in layers, with various connections among them. These modules can perform some basic transformations (usually non-linear ones) as data passes through them. Since there is a plethora of potential connections among these neurons, organizing them in a structured way (much like real neurons are organized in network in brain tissue), we can obtain a more robust and function form of these modules. This is what an artificial neural network is, in a nutshell.

In general, DL frameworks include tools for building a DL system, methods for testing it, and various other Extract, Transform, and Load (ETL) processes; when taken together, these framework components help you seamlessly integrate DL systems with the rest of your pipeline. We'll look at this in more detail later in this chapter.

Although deep learning systems share some similarities with machine learning systems, certain characteristics make them sufficiently distinct. For example, conventional machine learning systems tend to be simpler and have fewer options for training. DL systems are noticeably more sophisticated; they each have a set of *training algorithms,* along with several parameters regarding the systems' *architecture.* This is one of the reasons we consider them a distinct framework in data science.

DL systems also tend to be more autonomous than their machine counterparts. To some extent, DL systems can do their own *feature engineering.* More conventional systems tend to require more fine-tuning of the feature-set, and sometimes require *dimensionality reduction* to provide any decent results.

In addition, the *generalization* of conventional ML systems when provided with additional data generally don't improve as much as DL systems. This is also one of the key characteristics that makes DL systems a preferable option when *big data* is involved.

Finally, DL systems take longer to train and require more computational resources than conventional ML systems. This is due to their more sophisticated functionality. However, as the work of DL systems is easily *parallelizable,* modern computing architecture as well as cloud computing, benefit DL systems the most, compared to other predictive analytics systems.

How deep learning systems work

At their cores, all DL frameworks work similarly, particularly when it comes to the development of DL networks. First, a DL network consists of several neurons organized in layers; many of these are connected to other neurons in other layers. In the simplest DL network, connections take place only between neurons in adjacent layers.

The first layer of the network corresponds to the features of our dataset; the last layer corresponds to its outputs. In the case of *classification*, each class has its own node, with node values reflecting how confident the system is that a data point belongs to that class. The layers in the middle involve some combination of these features. Since they aren't visible to the end user of the network, they are described as *hidden* (see Figure 1).

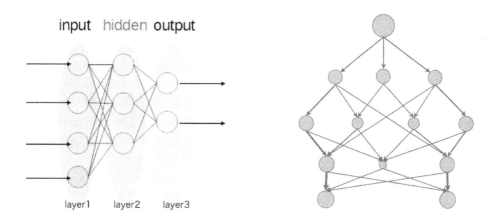

Figure 1. Depictions of a couple of simplified deep learning networks. There are often more hidden layers than seen in these examples. The number of neurons in the output layer can be arbitrary, depending on the *target variable*. Images created by *Richmanokada* and *AlexNet22*, respectively, and made available through CC licensing. The image on the right has been processed for additional comprehensiveness.

The connections among the nodes are weighted, indicating the contribution of each node to the nodes of the next layer it is connected to, in the next layer. The weights are initially randomized, when the network object is created, but are refined as the ANN is trained.

Moreover, each node contains a mathematical function that creates a transformation of the received signal, before it is passed to the next layer. This is referred to as the *transfer function* (also known as the *activation function*). The *sigmoid function* is the most well-known of these, but others include *softmax, tanh,* and *ReLU*. We'll delve more into these in a moment.

Furthermore, each layer has a *bias node,* which is a constant that appears unchanged on each layer. Just like all the other nodes, the bias node has a weight attached to its output. However, it has no transfer function. Its weighted value is simply added to the other nodes it is connected to, much like a constant c is added to a *regression* model in Statistics. The presence of such a term balances out any bias the other terms inevitably bring to the model, ensuring that the overall bias in the model is minimal. As the topic of bias is a very complex one, we recommend you check out some external resources[4] if you are not familiar with it.

Once the transformed inputs (features) and the biases arrive at the end of the DL network, they are compared with the *target variable*. The differences that inevitably occur are relayed back to the various nodes of the network, and the weights are changed accordingly. Then the whole process is repeated until the error margin of the outputs is within a certain predefined level, or until the maximum number of iterations is reached. Iterations of this process are often referred to as training *epochs,* and the whole process is intimately connected to the training algorithm used. In fact, the number of epochs used for training a DL network is often set as a parameter and it plays an important role in the ANN's performance.

All of the data entering a neuron (via connections with neurons of the previous layer, as well as the bias node) is summed, and then the transfer function is applied to the sum, so that the data flow from that node is $y = f(\Sigma(w_i x_i + b))$, where w_i is the weight of node i of the previous layer, and x_i its output, while b is the bias of that layer. Also, f() is the mathematical expression of the transfer function.

---

[4] A good starting point can be found at http://bit.ly/2vzKC30.

This relatively simple process is at the core of every ANN. The process is equivalent to that which takes place in a *perceptron* system—a rudimentary AI model that emulates the function of a single neuron. Although a perceptron system is never used in practice, it is the most basic element of an ANN, and the first system created using this paradigm.

The function of a single neuron is basically a single, predefined transformation of the data at hand. This can be viewed as a kind of meta-feature of the framework, as it takes a certain input x and after applying a (usually non-linear) function f() to it, x is transformed into something else, which is the neuron's output y.

While in the majority of cases one single meta-feature would be terrible at predicting the target variable, several of them across several layers can work together quite effectively – no matter how complex the mapping of the original features to the target variable. The downside is that such a system can easily *overfit*, which is why the training of an ANN doesn't end until the error is minimal (smaller than a predefined threshold).

This most rudimentary description of a DL network works for networks of the multi-layer perceptron type. Of course, there are several variants beyond this type. CNNs, for example, contain specialized layers with huge numbers of neurons, while RNNs have connections that go back to previous layers. Additionally, some training algorithms involve *pruning* nodes of the network to ensure that no overfitting takes place.

Once the DL network is trained, it can be used to make predictions about any data similar to the data it was trained on. Furthermore, its generalization capability is quite good, particularly if the data it is trained on is diverse. What's more, most DL networks are quite robust when it comes to noisy data, which sometimes helps them achieve even better generalization.

When it comes to classification problems, the performance of a DL system is improved by the class boundaries it creates. Although many conventional ML systems create straightforward boundary landscapes (e.g. rectangles or simple curves), a DL system creates a more sophisticated line around each class (reminiscent of the borders of certain counties in the US). This is because the DL system is trying to capture every bit of signal it is given in order to make fewer mistakes when classifying, boosting its raw performance. Of course, this highly complex mapping of the classes makes interpretation of the results a very challenging, if not unfeasible, task. More on that later in this chapter.

Main deep learning frameworks

Having knowledge of multiple DL frameworks gives you a better understanding of the AI field. You will not be limited by the capabilities of a specific framework. For example, some DL frameworks are geared towards a certain programming language, which may make focusing on just that framework an issue, since languages come and go. After all, things change very rapidly in technology, especially when it comes to software. What better way to shield yourself from any unpleasant developments than to be equipped with a diverse portfolio of DL know-how?

The main frameworks in DL include MXNet, TensorFlow, and Keras. Pytorch and Theano have also played an important role, but currently they are not as powerful or versatile as the aforementioned frameworks, which we will focus on in this book. Also, for those keen on the Julia language, there is the *Knet* framework, which to the best of our knowledge, is the only deep learning framework written in a high-level language mainly (in this case, Julia). You can learn more about it at its Github repository.[5]

MXNet is developed by Apache and it's Amazon's favorite framework. Some of Amazon's researchers have collaborated with researchers from the University of Washington to benchmark it and make it more widely known to the scientific community. We'll examine this framework in Chapter 3.

TensorFlow is probably the most well-known DL framework, partly because it has been developed by Google. As such, it is widely used in the industry and there are many courses and books discussing it. In Chapter 4 we'll delve into it more.

Keras is a high-level framework; it works on top of TensorFlow (as well as other frameworks like Theano). Its ease of use without losing flexibility or power makes it one of the favorite deep learning libraries today. Any data science enthusiast who wants to dig into the realm of deep learning can start using Keras with reasonably little effort. Moreover, Keras' seamless integrity with TensorFlow, plus the official support it gets from Google, have convinced many that Keras will be one of the long-lasting frameworks for deep learning models, while its corresponding library will continue to be maintained. We'll investigate it in detail in Chapter 5.

Main deep learning programming languages

As a set of techniques, DL is language-agnostic; any computer language can potentially be used to apply its methods and construct its data structures (the DL networks), even if each DL framework focuses on specific languages only.

---

[5] https://github.com/denizyuret/Knet.jl.

This is because it is more practical to develop frameworks that are compatible with certain languages, some programming languages are used more than others, such as Python. The fact that certain languages are more commonly used in data science plays an important role in language selection, too. Besides, DL is more of a data science framework nowadays anyway, so it is marketed to the data science community mainly, as part of Machine Learning (ML). This likely contributes to the confusion about what constitutes ML and AI these days.

Because of this, the language that dominates the DL domain is Python. This is also the reason why we use it in the DL part of this book. It is also one of the easiest languages to learn, even if you haven't done any programming before. However, if you are using a different language in your everyday work, there are DL frameworks that support other languages, such as Julia, *Scala*, R, JavaScript, Matlab, and Java. Julia is particularly useful for this sort of task as it is high-level (like Python, R, and Matlab), but also very fast (like any low-level language, including Java).

In addition, almost all the DL frameworks support C / C++, since they are usually written in C or its object-oriented counterpart. Note that all these languages access the DL frameworks through *APIs*, which take the form of packages in these languages. Therefore, in order to use a DL framework in your favorite language's environment, you must become familiar with the corresponding package, its classes, and its various functions. We'll guide you through all that in chapters 3 to 5 of this book.

How to leverage deep learning frameworks

Deep learning frameworks add value to AI and DS practitioners in various ways. The most important value-adding processes include *ETL* processes, building data models, and deploying these models. Beyond these main functions, a DL framework may offer other things that a data scientist can leverage to make their work easier. For example, a framework may include some visualization functionality, helping you produce some slick graphics to use in your report or presentation. As such, it's best to read up on each framework's documentation, becoming familiar with its capabilities to leverage it for your data science projects.

ETL processes

A DL framework can be helpful in fetching data from various sources, such as databases and files. This is a rather time-consuming process if done manually, so using a framework is very advantageous. The framework will also do some formatting on the data, so that you can start using it in your model without too much data engineering. However, doing some data processing of your own is always useful, particularly if you have some domain knowledge.

Building data models

The main function of a DL framework is to enable you to efficiently build data models. The framework facilitates the architecture design part, as well as all the data flow aspects of the ANN, including the training algorithm. In addition, the framework allows you to view the performance of the system as it is being trained, so that you gain insight about how likely it is to overfit.

Moreover, the DL framework takes care of all the testing required before the model is tested on different than the dataset it was trained on (new data). All this makes building and fine-tuning a DL data model a straightforward and intuitive process, empowering you to make a more informed choice about what model to use for your data science project.

Deploying data models

Model deployment is something that DL frameworks can handle, too, making movement through the data science pipeline swifter. This mitigates the risk of errors through this critical process, while also facilitating easy updating of the deployed model. All this enables the data scientist to focus more on the tasks that require more specialized or manual attention. For example, if you (rather than the DL model) worked on the feature engineering, you would have a greater awareness of exactly what is going into the model.

Deep learning methodologies and applications

Deep learning is a very broad AI category, encompassing several data science methodologies through its various systems. As we have seen, for example, it can be successfully used in classification—if the output layer of the network is built with the same number of neurons as the number of classes in the dataset. When DL is applied to problems with the regression methodology, things are simpler, as a single neuron in the output layer is enough. *Reinforcement learning* is another methodology where DL is used; along with the other two methodologies, it forms the set of *supervised learning,* a broad methodology under the predictive analytics umbrella (see Appendix B).

DL is also used for dimensionality reduction, which (in this case) comprises a set of meta-features that are usually developed by an *autoencoder* system (see Appendix C for more details on this kind of DL network). This approach to dimensionality reduction is also more efficient than the traditional statistical ones, which are computationally expensive when the number of features is remarkably high. *Clustering* is another methodology where deep learning can be used, with the proper changes in the ANN's structure and data flow. Clustering and dimensionality reduction are the most popular *unsupervised learning* methodologies in data science and provide a lot of value when exploring a dataset. Beyond these data science methodologies involving DL, there are others that are more specialized and require some domain expertise. We'll talk about some of them more, shortly.

There are many applications of deep learning. Some are more established or general, while others are more specialized or novel. Since DL is still a new tool, its applications in the data science world remain works in progress, so keep an open mind about this matter. After all, the purpose of all AI systems is to be as universally applicable as possible, so the list of applications is only going to grow.

For the time being, DL is used in complex problems where high-accuracy predictions are required. These could be datasets with high dimensionality and/or highly non-linear patterns. In the case of high-dimensional datasets that need to be summarized into a more compact form with fewer dimensions, DL is a highly effective tool for the job. Also, since the very beginning of its creation, DL has been applied to image, sound, and video analytics, with a focus on images. Such data is quite difficult to process otherwise; the tools used before DL could only help so much, and developing those features manually was a very time-consuming process.

Moving on to more niche applications, DL is widely used in various *natural language processing (NLP)* methods. This includes all kinds of data related to everyday text, such as that found in articles, books, and even social media posts. Where it is important to identify any positive or negative attitudes in the text, we use a methodology called *"sentiment analysis,"* which offers a fertile ground for many DL systems. There are also DL networks that perform text prediction, which is common in many mobile devices and some text editors. More advanced DL systems manage to link images to captions by mapping these images to words that are relevant and that form sentences. Such advanced applications of DL include chatbots, in which the AI system both creates text and understands the text it is given. Also, applications like text summarization are under the NLP umbrella too and DL contributes to them significantly. Some DL applications are more advanced or domain-specific – so much so that they require a tremendous amount of data and computing power to work. However, as computing becomes more readily available, these are bound to become more accessible in the short term.

Assessing a deep learning framework

DL frameworks make it easy and efficient to employ DL in a data science project. Of course, part of the challenge is deciding which framework to use. Because not all DL frameworks are built equal, there are factors to keep in mind when comparing or evaluating these frameworks.

The number of languages supported by a framework is especially important. Since programming languages are particularly fluid in the data science world, it is best to have your language bases covered in the DL framework you plan to use. What's more, having multiple languages support in a DL framework enables the formation of a more diverse data science team, with each member having different specific programming expertise.

You must also consider the raw performance of the DL systems developed by the framework in question. Although most of these systems use the same low-level language on the back end, not all of them are fast. There may also be other overhead costs involved. As such, it's best to do your due diligence before investing your time in a DL framework—particularly if your decision affects other people in your organization.

Furthermore, consider the ETL processes supporting a DL framework. Not all frameworks are good at ETL, which is both inevitable and time-consuming in a data science pipeline. Again, any inefficiencies of a DL framework in this aspect are not going to be advertised; you must do some research to uncover them yourself.

Finally, the user community and documentation around a DL framework are important things, too. Naturally, the documentation of the framework is going to be helpful, though in some cases it may leave much to be desired. If there is a healthy community of users for the DL framework you are considering, things are bound to be easier when learning its more esoteric aspects—as well as when you need to troubleshoot issues that may arise.

Interpretability

Interpretability is the capability of a model to be understood in terms of its functionality and its results. Although interpretability is often a given with conventional data science systems, it is a pain point of every DL system. This is because every DL model is a "black box," offering little to no explanation for why it yields the results it does. Unlike the framework itself, whose various modules and their functionality is clear, the models developed by these frameworks are convoluted graphs. There is no comprehensive explanation as to how the inputs you feed them turn into the outputs they yield.

Although obtaining an accurate result through such a method may be enticing, it is quite hard to defend, especially when the results are controversial or carry a demographic bias. The reason for a demographic bias has to do with the data, by the way, so no number of bias nodes in the DL networks can fix that, since a DL network's predictions can only be as good as the data used to train it. Also, the fact that we have no idea how the predictions correspond to the inputs allows biased predictions to slip through unnoticed.

However, this lack of interpretability may be resolved in the future. This may require a new approach to them, but if it's one thing that the progress of AI system has demonstrated over the years, it is that innovations are still possible and that new architectures of models are still being discovered. Perhaps one of the newer DL systems will have interpretability as one of its key characteristics.

Model maintenance

Maintenance is essential to every data science model. This entails updating or even upgrading a model in production, as new data becomes available. Alternatively, the assumptions of the problem may change; when this happens, model maintenance is also needed. In a DL setting, model maintenance usually involves retraining the DL network. If the retrained model doesn't perform well enough, more significant changes may be considered such as changing the architecture or the training parameters. Whatever the case, this whole process is largely straightforward and not too time-consuming.

How often model maintenance is required depends on the dataset and the problem in general. Whatever the case, it is good to keep the previous model available too when doing major changes, in case the new model has unforeseen issues. Also, the whole model maintenance process can be automated to some extent, at least the offline part, when the model is retrained as new data is integrated with the original dataset.

When to use DL over conventional data science systems

Deciding when to use a DL system instead of a conventional method is an important task. It is easy to be enticed by the new and exciting features of DL, and to use it for all kinds of data science problems. However, not all problems require DL. Sometimes, the extra performance of DL is not worth the extra resources required. In cases where conventional data science systems fail, or don't offer any advantage (like interpretability), DL systems may be preferable.

Complex problems with lots of variables and cases with non-linear relationships between the features and the target variables are great matches for a DL framework.

If there is an abundance of data, and the main objective is good raw performance in the model, a DL system is typically preferable. This is particularly true if computational resources are not a concern, since a DL system requires quite a lot of them, especially during its training phase. Whatever the case, it's good to consider alternatives before setting off to build a DL model. While these models are incredibly versatile and powerful, sometimes simpler systems are good enough.

Summary

- Deep Learning is a particularly important aspect of AI, and has found a lot of applications in data science.

- Deep Learning employs a certain kind of AI system called an Artificial Neural Networks (or ANN). An ANN is a graph-based system involving a series of (usually non-linear) operations, whereby the original features are transformed into a few meta-features capable of predicting the target variable more accurately than the original features.

- The main frameworks in DL are MXNet, TensorFlow, and Keras, though Pytorch and Theano also play roles in the whole DL ecosystem. Also, Knet is an interesting alternative for those using Julia primarily.

- There are various programming languages used in DL, including Python, Julia, Scala, Javascript, R, and C / C++. Python is the most popular.

- A DL framework offers diverse functionality, including ETL processes, building data models, deploying and evaluating models, and other functions like creating visuals.

- A DL system can be used in various data science methodologies, including Classification, Regression, Reinforcement Learning, Dimensionality Reduction, Clustering, and Sentiment Analysis.

- Classification, regression, and reinforcement learning are supervised learning methodologies, while dimensionality reduction and clustering are unsupervised.

- Applications of DL include making high-accuracy predictions for complex problems; summarizing data into a more compact form; analyzing images, sound, or video; natural language processing and sentiment analysis; text prediction; linking images to captions; chatbots; and text summarization.

- A DL framework needs to be assessed on various metrics (not just popularity). Such factors include the programming languages it supports, its raw performance, how well it handles ETL processes, the strength of its documentation and user communities, and the need for future maintenance.

- It is not currently very easy to interpret DL results and trace them back to specific features (i.e. DL results currently have low *interpretability*).

- Giving more weight to raw performance or interpretability can help you decide whether a DL system or conventional data science system is ideal for your particular problem. Other factors, like the amount of computational resources at our disposal, are also essential for making this decision.

## CHAPTER 2

AI Methodologies Beyond Deep Learning

As we've seen, deep learning is a key aspect of most robust AI systems—but it's not the only way to use AI. This chapter covers some alternatives to deep learning. Even if these methods are not as popular as DL methods, they can be very useful in certain scenarios. We'll take a look at the two main methodologies – optimization and fuzzy logic – as well as some less well-known methods such as *artificial creativity*. We'll cover new trends in AI methodologies. Finally, we'll explore some useful considerations to leverage these methods and make the most out of them for your data science projects.

Many of the AI methodologies alternative to DL don't use ANNs of any kind, but rely on other systems that exhibit a certain level of intelligence. As some such systems don't use an obscure graph for making their predictions (like ANNs do) they are more transparent than DL, making them useful when interpreting results. Most of these alternative AI methodologies have been around for a few decades now, so there is plenty of support behind them, making them reliable resources overall. Others are generally newer, but are quite robust and reliable nevertheless.

Since the field of AI is rapidly evolving, these alternatives to DL may become even more relevant over the next few years. After all, many data science problems involve optimizing a function.

Among the various alternative AI methodologies out there, the ones that are more suitable for data science work can be classified under the *optimization* umbrella. However, fuzzy logic systems may be useful, even though they apply mainly to low-dimensionality datasets, as we'll see later. Optimization, on the other hand, involves all kinds of datasets, and is often used within other data science systems.

Optimization

Optimization is the process of finding the maximum or minimum of a given function (also known as a *fitness function)*, by calculating the best values for its variables (also known as a "solution"). Despite the simplicity of this definition, it is not an easy process; often involves restrictions, as well as complex relationships among the various variables. Even though some functions can be optimized using some mathematical process, most functions we encounter in data science are not as simple, requiring a more advanced technique.

Optimization systems (or *optimizers*, as they are often referred to) aim to optimize in a systematic way, oftentimes using a heuristics-based approach. Such an approach enables the AI system to use a macro level concept as part of its low-level calculations, accelerating the whole process and making it more light-weight. After all, most of these systems are designed with scalability in mind, so the heuristic approach is most practical.

Importance of optimization

Optimization is especially important in many data science problems— particularly those involving a lot of variables that need to be fine-tuned, or cases where the conventional tools don't seem to work. In order to tackle more complex problems, beyond classical methodologies, optimization is essential. Moreover, optimization is useful for various data engineering tasks such as *feature selection*, in cases where maintaining a high degree of interpretability is desired. We'll investigate the main applications of optimizers in data science later in this chapter.

Optimization systems overview

There are different kinds of optimization systems. The most basic ones have been around the longest. These are called "deterministic optimizers," and they tend to yield the best possible solution for the problem at hand. That is, the absolute maximum or minimum of the fitness function. Since they are quite time-consuming and cannot handle large-scale problems, these deterministic optimizers are usually used for applications where the number of variables is relatively small. A classic example of such an optimizer is the one used for least squared error regression—a simple method to figure out the optimal line that fits a set of data points, in a space with relatively small dimensionality.

In addition to deterministic optimizers, there are *stochastic* optimizers, which more closely fit the definition of AI. After all, most of these are based on natural phenomena, such as the movement of the members of a *swarm*, or the way a metal melts. The main advantage of these methods is that they are very efficient. Although they usually don't yield the absolute maximum or minimum of the function they are trying to optimize, their solutions are good enough for all practical purposes (even if they vary slightly every time you run the optimizer). Stochastic optimizers also scale very well, so they are ideal for complex problems involving many variables. In this book we will focus on some of these stochastic optimization methods.

Programming languages for optimization

Optimization is supported by most programming languages in terms of libraries, like the *Optim* and *JuMP* packages in Julia. However, each algorithm is simple enough so that you can code it yourself, if you cannot find an available "off-the-shelf" function. In this book we'll examine the main algorithms for advanced optimization and how they are implemented in Julia. We chose this programming language because it combines ease of use and high execution speed. Remember that all the code is available in the Docker environment that accompanies this book.

Fuzzy inference systems

Fuzzy logic (FL) is a methodology designed to emulate the human capacity of imprecise or approximate reasoning. This ability to judge under uncertainty was previously considered strictly human, but FL has made it possible for machines, too.

Despite its name, there is nothing unclear about the outputs of fuzzy logic. This is because fuzzy logic is an extension of classical logic, when partial truths are included to extend bivalued logic (true or false) to a multivalued logic (degrees of truth between true and false).

According to its creator, Professor Zadeh, the ultimate goal of fuzzy logic is to form the theoretical foundation for reasoning about imprecise propositions (also known as "approximate reasoning"). Over the past couple decades, FL has gained ground and become regarded as one of the most promising AI methodologies.

A FL system contains a series of mappings corresponding to the various features of the data at hand. This system contains terms that make sense to us, such as high-low, hot-cold, and large-medium-small, terms that may appear fuzzy since there are no clear-cut boundaries among them. Also, these attributes are generally relative and require some context to become explicit, through a given mapping between each term and some number that the system can use in its processes. This mapping is described mathematically through a set of membership functions, graphically taking the form of triangles, trapezoids, or even curves. This way something somewhat abstract like "large" can take very specific dimensions in the form of "how large on a scale of 0 to 1" it is. The process of coding data into these states is called *fuzzification*.

Once all the data is coded in this manner, the various mappings are merged together through logical operators, such as inference rules (for example, "If A and B then C," where A and B correspond to states of two different features and C to the target variable). The result is a new membership function describing this complex relationship, usually depicted as a polygon. This is then turned into a crisp value, through one of various methods, in a process called *defuzzification*. Since this whole process is graphically accessible to the user, and the terms used are borrowed from human language, the result is always something clear-cut and interpretable (given some understanding of how FL works).

Interestingly, FL has also been used in conjunction with ANNs to form what are referred to as *neuro-fuzzy* systems. Instead of having a person create the membership functions by hand, a FL system can make use of the optimization method in a neural network's training algorithm to calculate them on the fly. This whole process and the data structure that it entails take the form of an automated fuzzy system, combining the best of both worlds.

Why systems based on fuzzy logic are still relevant

Although FL was originally developed with a certain types of engineering systems in mind such as Control Systems, its ease of use and low cost of implementation has made it relevant as an AI methodology across a variety of other fields, including data science.

What's more, fuzzy systems are very accessible, especially when automated through optimization for their membership functions (such as the neuro-fuzzy systems mentioned previously). Such a system employs a set of FL rules (which are created based on the data) to infer the target variable. These systems are called Fuzzy Inference Systems, or FISs.

The main advantage of this FIS approach is that it is transparent—a big plus if you want to defend your results to the project stakeholders. The transparency of a FIS makes the whole problem more understandable, enabling you to figure out which features are more relevant.

In addition, a FIS can be used in conjunction with custom-made rules based on an expert's knowledge. This is particularly useful if you are looking at upgrading a set of heuristic rules using AI. Certain larger companies that are planning to use data science to augment their existing systems are likely to be interested in such a solution.

Downside of fuzzy inference systems

Despite all the merits of FIS, these AI systems don't always meet the expectations of modern data science projects. Specifically, when the dimensionality of the data at hand is quite large, the number of rules produced increases exponentially, making these systems too large for any practical purposes. Of course, you can mitigate this issue with an autoencoder or a statistical process, like PCA or ICA, that creates a smaller set of features.

However, when you do this, the whole interpretability benefit of FIS goes out the window. Why? With a reduced feature set, the relationship with the original features (and the semantic meaning they carry) is warped. As such, it is very difficult to reconstruct meaning; the new features will require a different interpretation if they are to be meaningful. This is not always feasible.

Nevertheless, for datasets of smaller dimensionality, a FIS is a worthwhile alternative, even if it's not a particularly popular one. We'll explore Fuzzy Logic and FIS more in Chapter 11, where we'll discuss alternative AI methodologies.

Artificial creativity

Artificial creativity (AC) is a relatively new methodology of AI, where new information is created based on relevant data it has been trained on. Its applications span across various domains, including most of the arts, as well as industrial design, and even data science.

This kind of AI methodology makes use of a specialized DL network that is trained to develop new data that retains some characteristics of the data it was trained on. When you feed such a specialized AI system some image data, and it's been trained on the artwork of a particular painter, it will produce new "artwork" that makes use of the images it is fed, but using the painting patterns of the artist it is trained to emulate. The results may not win any art prizes, but they are certainly interesting and original!

It is particularly fascinating when an AC system creates poetry, based on the verse of certain poets. The results can be indistinguishable from human-written verse. Take for example the following piece of verse by the AI poet Deep Gimble I:[6]

> *Madness in her face and i*
> *the world that I had seen*
> *and when my soul shall be to see the night to be the same and*
> *I am all the world and the day that is the same and a day I had been*
> *a young little woman I am in a dream that you were in*
> *a moment and my own heart in her face of a great world*
> *and she said the little day is a man of a little*
> *a little one of a day of my heart that has been in a dream.*

In data science, AC can aid in the creation of new data, which is quite useful in certain cases. This new data may not be particularly helpful as an expansion of the training set for that ANN, but it can be especially useful in other ways. For example, if the original data is sensitive like medical data, and contains too much *personally identifiable information (PII),* you can generate new data using AC that, although very similar to the original data, cannot be mapped back to a real individual.

In addition, data created from an AC system can be useful for different data models—perhaps as a new test set or even part of their training set. This way it can offer the potential for better generalization for these models, as there is more data available for them to train or test on. This can be particularly useful in domains where labeled data is hard to come by or is expensive to generate otherwise.

---

[6] http://bit.ly/2Js4CKd.

Additional AI methodologies

Beyond all the AI methodologies we've discussed so far, there exist several others worth noting. These systems also have a role to play in data science, while their similarities to DL systems make them easier to comprehend. Also, as the AI field is constantly expanding, it's good to be aware of all the new methodologies that pop up.

The Extreme Learning Machine (or ELM) is an example of an alternative AI methodology that hasn't yet received the attention it deserves. Although they are architecturally like DL networks, ELMs are quite distinct in the way they are trained. In fact, their training is so unconventional that some people considered the whole approach borderline unscientific (the professor who came up with ELMs most recently has received a lot of criticism from other academics).

Instead of optimizing all the weights across the network, ELMs focus on just the connections of the two last layers—namely the last set of meta-features and their outputs. The rest of the weights maintain their initial random values from the beginning. Because the focus is solely on just the optimized weights of the last layers, this optimization is extremely fast and very precise.

As a result, ELMs are the fastest network-based methodology out there, and their performance is quite decent too. What's more, they are quite unlikely to overfit, which is another advantage. Despite its counter-intuitive approach, an ELM system does essentially the same thing as a conventional DL system; instead of optimizing all the meta-features it creates, though, it focuses on optimizing the way they work together to form a predictive analytics model. We'll talk more about ELMs in Chapter 11.

Another new alternative AI methodology is Capsule Networks (CapsNets). Although the CapsNet should be regarded as a member of the deep learning methods family, its architecture and its optimization training method are quite novel. CapsNets try to capture the relative relationships between the objects within a relevant context. A CNN model that achieves high performance in image recognition tasks may not necessarily be able to identify the same object from different angles. CapsNets, though, capture those kinds of contextual relationships quite well. Their performance on some tasks has already surpassed the leading models by about 45%, which is quite astonishing. Considering their promising future, we dedicate a section in Chapter 11 to discussing CapsNets.

Self-organizing Maps (SOMs) are a special type of AI system. Although they are also ANNs of sorts, they are unique in function. SOMs offer a way to map the feature space into a two-dimensional grid, so that it can be better visualized afterwards. Since it doesn't make use of a target variable, a SOM is an unsupervised learning methodology; as such, it is ideal for *data exploration*.

SOMs have been successfully applied in various domains, such as meteorology, oceanography, oil and gas exploration, and project prioritization. One key difference SOMs have from other ANNs is that their learning is based on competition instead of error correction. Also, their architecture is quite different, as their various nodes are only connected to the input layer with no lateral connections. This unique design was first introduced by Professor Kohonen, which is why SOMs are also referred to as "Kohonen Maps."

The *Generative Adversarial Network (GAN)* is a very interesting type of AI methodology, geared towards optimizing a DL network in a rather creative way. A GAN comprises two distinct ANNs. One is for learning, and the other is for "breaking" the first one – finding cases where the predictions of the first ANN are off. These systems are comparable to the "white hat" hackers of cybersecurity.

In essence, the second ANN creates increasingly more demanding challenges for the first ANN, thereby constantly improving its generalization (even with a limited amount of data). GANs are used for simulations as well as data science problems. Their main field of application is astronomy, where a somewhat limited quantity of images and videos of the cosmos is available to use in training. The idea of GANs has been around for over a decade, but has only recently managed to gain popularity; this is largely due to the amount of computational resources demanded by such a system (just like any other DL-related AI system). A more detailed description of GANs is available in Appendix D, while in Chapter 9 we'll also revisit this topic.

Artificial Emotional Intelligence (AEI) is another kind of AI that's novel on both the methodological as well as the application levels. The goal of AEI is to facilitate an understanding of the emotional context of data (which is usually text-based) and to assess it just like a human. Applications of AEI are currently limited to comprehension; in the future, though, more interactive systems could provide a smoother interface between humans and machines. There is an intersect between AEI and ANNs, but some aspects of AEI make use of other kinds of ML systems on the back end.

Glimpse into the future

While the field of AI expands in various directions, making it hard to speculate about how it will evolve, there is one common drawback to most of the AI systems used today: a lack of interpretability. As such, it is quite likely that some future AI system will address this matter, providing a more comprehensive result, or at least some information as to how the result came about (something like a rationale for each prediction), all while maintaining the scalability of modern AI systems.

A more advanced AI system of the future will likely have a network structure, just like current DL systems—though it may be quite different architecturally.

Such a system would be able to learn with fewer data points (possibly assisted by a GAN), as well as generate new data (just like variational autoencoders).

Could an AI system learn to build new AI systems? It is possible, however the limitation of excessive resources required for such a task has made it feasible only for cloud-based systems. Google may showcase its progress in this area in what it refers to as *Automated Machine Learning (AutoML)*.

So, if you were to replicate this task with your own system, who is to say that the AI-created AI would be better than what you yourself would have built? Furthermore, would you be able to pinpoint its shortcomings, which may be quite subtle and obscure? After all, an AI system requires a lot of effort to make sure that its results are not just accurate but also useful, addressing the end-user's needs. You can imagine how risky it would be to have an AI system built that you know nothing about!

However, all this is just an idea of a potential evolutionary course, since AI can always evolve in unexpected ways. Fortunately, with all the popularity of AI systems today, if something new and better comes along, you'll probably find out about it sooner rather than later.

Perhaps for things like that it's best to stop and think about the why's instead of focusing only on the how's, since as many science and industry experts have warned us, AI is a high-risk endeavor and needs to be handled carefully and always with fail-safes set in place. For example, although it's fascinating and in some cases important to think about how we can develop AIs that improve themselves, it's also crucial to understand what implications this may have and plan for AI safety matters beforehand. Also, prioritizing certain characteristics of an AI system (e.g. interpretability, ease of use, having limited issues in the case of malfunction, etc.) over raw performance, may provide more far-reaching benefits. After all, isn't improving our lives in the long-term the reason why we have AI in the first place?

About the methods

It is not hard to find problems that can be tackled with optimization. For example, you may be looking at an optimum configuration of a marketing process to minimize the total cost, or to maximize the number of people reached. Although data science can lend some aid in solving such a problem, at the end of the day, you'll need to employ an optimizer to find a true solution to a problem like this.

Furthermore, optimization can help in data engineering, too. Some feature selection methods, for instance, use optimization to keep only the features that work well together. There are also cases of *feature fusion* that employ optimization (although few people use this method, since it sacrifices some interpretability of the model that makes use of these meta-features).

In addition, when building a custom predictive analytics system combining other *classifiers* or *regressors*, you often need to maximize the overall accuracy rate (or some other performance metric). To do this, you must figure out the best parameters for each module (i.e. the ones that optimize a certain performance metric for the corresponding model), and consider the weights of each module's output in the overall decision rule for the final output of the system that comprises of all these modules. This work really requires an optimizer, since often the number of variables involved is considerable.

In general, if you are tackling a predictive analytics problem and you have a dataset whose dimensionality you have reduced through feature selection, it can be effectively processed through a FIS. In addition, if interpretability is a key requirement for your data model, using a FIS is a good strategy to follow. Finally, if you already have a set of heuristic rules at your disposal from an existing predictive analytics system, then you can use a FIS to merge those rules with some new ones that the FIS creates. This way, you won't have to start from square one when developing your solution.

Novel AI systems tend to be less predictable and, as a result, somewhat unreliable. They may work well for a certain dataset, but that performance may not hold true with other datasets.

That's why it is critical to try out different AI systems before settling on one to use as your main data model. In many cases, optimizing a certain AI system may yield better performance, despite the time and resources it takes to optimize. Striking the balance between exploring various alternatives and digging deeper into existing ones is something that comes about with experience.

Moreover, it's a good idea to set your project demands and user requirements beforehand. Knowing what is needed can make the selection of your AI system (or if you are more adventurous, your design of a new one) much easier and more straightforward. For example, if you state early on that interpretability is more important than performance, this will affect which model you decide to use. Make sure you understand what you are looking for in an AI system from the beginning, as this is bound to help you significantly in making the optimal choice.

Although AI systems have a lot to offer in all kinds of data science problems, they are not panaceas. If the data at your disposal is not of high veracity, meaning not of good quality or reliability, no AI system can remedy that. All AI systems function based on the data we train them with; if the training data is very noisy, biased, or otherwise problematic, their generalizations are not going to be any better.

This underlines the importance of data engineering and utilizing data from various sources, thereby maximizing your chances of creating a robust and useful data model. This is also why it's always good to always keep a human in the loop when it comes to data science projects—even (or perhaps especially) when they evolve AI.

Summary

- Optimization is an AI-related process for finding the maximum or minimum of a given function, by tweaking the values for its variables. It is an integral part of many other systems (including ANNs) and consists of deterministic and stochastic systems.

- Optimization systems (or "optimizers," as they are often called) can be implemented in all programming languages, since their main algorithms are fairly straightforward.

- Fuzzy Logic (FL) is an AI methodology that attempts to model imprecise data as well as uncertainty. Systems employing FL are referred to as Fuzzy Inference Systems (FIS). These systems involve the development and use of fuzzy rules, which automatically link features to the target variable. A FIS is great for datasets of small dimensionality, since it doesn't scale well as the number of features increases.

- Artificial creativity (AC) is an AI methodology of sorts that creates new information based on patterns derived from the data it is fed. It has many applications in the arts and industrial design. This methodology could also be useful in data science, through the creation of new data points for sensitive datasets (for example, where data privacy is important).

- Artificial Emotional Intelligence (AEI) is another alternative AI, emulating human emotions. Currently its applications are limited to comprehension.

- Although speculative, if a truly novel AI methodology were to arise in the near future, it would probably combine the characteristics of existing AI systems, with an emphasis on interpretability.

- Even though theoretically possible, an AI system that can design and build other AI systems is not a trivial task. A big part of this involves the excessive risks of using such a system, since we would have little control over the result.

- It's important to understand the subtle differences between all these methodologies, as well as their various limitations. Most importantly, for data science, there is no substitute for high veracity data.

Building a DL Network Using MXNet

We'll begin our in-depth examinations of the DL frameworks with that which seems one of the most promising: Apache's MXNet. We'll cover its core components including the *Gluon* interface, *NDArrays*, and the MXNet package in Python. You will learn how you can save your work like the networks you trained in data files, and some other useful things to keep in mind about MXNet.

MXNet supports a variety of programming languages through its API, most of which are useful for data science. Languages like Python, Julia, Scala, R, Perl, and C++ have their own wrappers of the MXNet system, which makes them easily integrated with your pipeline.

Also, MXNet allows for parallelism, letting you take full advantage of your machine's additional hardware resources, such as extra CPUs and GPUs. This makes MXNet quite fast, which is essential when tackling computationally heavy problems, like the ones found in most DL applications.

Interestingly, the DL systems you create in MXNet can be deployed on all kinds of computer platforms, including smart devices. This is possible through a process called *amalgamation*, which ports a whole system into a single file that can then be executed as a standalone program. Amalgamation in MXNet was created by Jack Deng, and involves the development of .cc files, which use the BLAS library as their only dependency. Files like this tend to be quite large (more than 30000 lines long). There is also the option of compiling .h files using a program called *emscripten*. This program is independent of any library, and can be used by other programming languages with the corresponding API.

Finally, there exist several tutorials for MXNet, should you wish to learn more about its various functions. Because MXNet is an open-source project, you can even create your own tutorial, if you are so inclined. What's more, it is a cross-platform tool, running on all major operating systems. MXNet has been around long enough that it is a topic of much research, including a well-known academic paper by Chen et al.[7]

Core components

Gluon interface

Gluon is a simple interface for all your DL work using MXNet. You install it on your machine just like any Python library:

```
pip install mxnet --pre --user
```

The main selling point of Gluon is that it is straightforward. It offers an abstraction of the whole network building process, which can be intimidating for people new to the craft. Also, Gluon is very fast, not adding any significant overhead to the training of your DL system. Moreover, Gluon can handle dynamic graphs, offering some malleability in the structure of the ANNs created. Finally, Gluon has an overall flexible structure, making the development process for any ANN less rigid.

---

[7] https://bit.ly/2uweNb0.

Naturally, for Gluon to work, you must have MXNet installed on your machine (although you don't need to if you are using the Docker container provided with this book). This is achieved using the familiar pip command:

```
pip install mxnet --pre --user
```

Because of its utility and excellent integration with MXNet, we'll be using Gluon throughout this chapter, as we explore this DL framework. However, to get a better understanding of MXNet, we'll first briefly consider how you can use some of its other functions (which will come in handy for one of the case studies we examine later).

NDArrays

The NDArray is a particularly useful *data structure* that's used throughout an MXNet project. NDArrays are essentially NumPy arrays, but with the added capability of asynchronous CPU processing. They are also compatible with distributed cloud architectures, and can even utilize automatic differentiation, which is particularly useful when training a deep learning system, but NDArrays can be effectively used in other ML applications too. NDArrays are part of the MXNet package, which we will examine shortly. You can import the NDArrays module as follows:

```
from mxnet import nd
```

To create a new NDArray consisting of 4 rows and 5 columns, for example, you can type the following:

```
nd.empty((4, 5))
```

The output will differ every time you run it, since the framework will allocate whatever value it finds in the parts of the memory that it allocates to that array. If you want the NDArray to have just zeros instead, type:

```
nd.zeros((4, 5))
```

To find the number of rows and columns of a variable having an NDArray assigned to it, you need to use the *.shape* function, just like in NumPy:

```
x = nd.empty((2, 7))
x.shape
```

Finally, if you want to find to total number of elements in an NDArray, you use the *.size* function:

```
x.size
```

The operations in an NDArray are just like the ones in NumPy, so we won't elaborate on them here. Contents are also accessed in the same way, through indexing and slicing.

Should you want to turn an NDArray into a more familiar data structure from the NumPy package, you can use the *asnumpy()* function:

```
y = x.asnumpy()
```

The reverse can be achieved using the *array()* function:

```
z = nd.array(y)
```

One of the distinguishing characteristics of NDArrays is that they can assign different computational contexts to different arrays—either on the CPU or on a GPU attached to your machine (this is referred to as *"context"* when discussing about NDArrays). This is made possible by the *ctx* parameter in all the package's relevant functions. For example, when creating an empty array of zeros that you want to assign to the first GPU, simply type:

```
a = nd.zeros(shape=(5,5), ctx=mx.gpu(0))
```

Of course, the data assigned to a particular processing unit is not set in stone. It is easy to copy data to a different location, linked to a different processing unit, using the *copyto()* function:

```
y = x.copyto(mx.gpu(1)) # copy the data of NDArray x to the 2nd
    GPU
```

You can find the context of a variable through the *.context* attribute:

```
print(x.context)
```

It is often more convenient to define the context of both the data and the models, using a separate variable for each. For example, say that your DL project uses data that you want to be processed by the CPU, and a model that you prefer to be handled by the first GPU. In this case, you'd type something like:

```
DataCtx = mx.cpu()
ModelCtx = mx.gpu(0)
```

MXNet package in Python

The MXNet package (or "mxnet," with all lower-case letters, when typed in Python), is a very robust and self-sufficient library in Python. MXNet provides deep learning capabilities through the MXNet framework. Importing this package in Python is fairly straightforward:

```
import mxnet as mx
```

If you want to perform some additional processes that make the MXNet experience even better, it is highly recommended that you first install the following packages on your computer:

- *graphviz* (ver. 0.8.1 or later)
- *requests* (ver. 2.18.4 or later)
- *numpy* (ver. 1.13.3 or later)

You can learn more about the MXNet package through the corresponding GitHub repository.[8]

MXNet in action

Now let's take a look at what we can do with MXNet, using Python, on a Docker image with all the necessary software already installed. We'll begin with a brief description of the datasets we'll use, and then proceed to a couple specific DL applications using that data (namely classification and regression). Upon mastering these, you can explore some more advanced DL systems of this framework on your own.

Datasets description

In this section we'll introduce two synthetic datasets that we prepared to demonstrate classification and regression methods on them. First dataset is for classification, and the other for regression. The reason we use synthetic datasets in these exercises to maximize our understanding of the data, so that we can evaluate the results of the DL systems independent of data quality.

The first dataset comprises 4 variables, 3 features, and 1 labels variable. With 250,000 data points, it is adequately large for a DL network to work with. Its small dimensionality makes it ideal for visualization (see Figure 2). It is also made to have a great deal of non-linearity, making it a good challenge for any data model (though not too hard for a DL system). Furthermore, classes 2 and 3 of this dataset are close enough to be confusing, but still distinct. This makes them a good option for a clustering application, as we'll see later.

---

[8] https://github.com/apache/incubator-mxnet

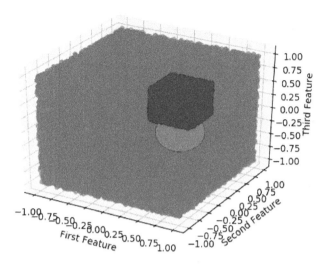

Figure 2: A graphical representation of the first dataset to be used in these examples. The different colors correspond to the different classes of the dataset. Although the three classes are defined clearly, figuring out in which one of them an unknown data point belongs is non-linear. This is due to the presence of the spherical class, making the whole problem challenging enough to render a DL approach to it relevant.

The second dataset is somewhat larger, comprising 21 variables—20 of which are the features used to predict the last, which is the target variable. With 250,000 data points, again, it is ideal for a DL system. Note that only 10 of the 20 features are relevant to the target variable (which is a combination of these 10). A bit of noise is added to the data to make the whole problem a bit more challenging. The remaining 10 features are just random data that must be filtered out by the DL model. Relevant or not, this dataset has enough features altogether to render a dimensionality reduction application worthwhile. Naturally, due to its dimensionality, we cannot plot this dataset.

Loading a dataset into an NDArray

Let's now take a look at how we can load a dataset in MXNet, so that we can process it with a DL model later on. First let's start with setting some parameters:

```
DataCtx = mx.cpu() # assign context of the data used
BatchSize = 64 # batch parameter for dataloader object
r = 0.8 # ratio of training data
nf = 3 # number of features in the dataset (for the
    classification problem)
```

Now, we can import the data like we'd normally do in a conventional DS project, but this time store it in NDArrays instead of Pandas or NumPy arrays:

```
with open("../data/data1.csv") as f:
    data_raw = f.read()
lines = data_raw.splitlines() # split the data into separate
    lines
ndp = len(lines) # number of data points
X = nd.zeros((ndp, nf), ctx=data_ctx)
Y = nd.zeros((ndp, 1), ctx=data_ctx)
for i, line in enumerate(lines):
tokens = line.split()
Y[i] = int(tokens[0])
for token in tokens[1:]:
        index = int(token[:-2]) - 1
        X[i, index] = 1
```

Now we can split the data into a *training set* and a *testing set,* so that we can use it both to build and to validate our classification model:

```
import numpy as np # we'll be needing this package as well
n = np.round(N * r) # number of training data points
train = data[:n, ] # training set partition
test = data[(n + 1):,] # testing set partition
data_train =
    gluon.data.DataLoader(gluon.data.ArrayDataset(train[:,:3],
                                        train[:,3]),
        batch_size=BatchSize, shuffle=True)
data_test =
    gluon.data.DataLoader(gluon.data.ArrayDataset(test[:,:3],
                                        test[:,3]),
        batch_size=BatchSize, shuffle=True)
```

We'll then need to repeat the same process to load the second dataset—this time using *data2.csv* as the source file. Also, to avoid confusion with the dataloader objects of dataset 1, you can name the new dataloaders *data_train2* and *data_test2*, respectively.

Classification

Now let's explore how we can use this data to build an MLP system that can discern the different classes within the data we have prepared. For starters, let's see how to do this using the mxnet package on its own; then we'll examine how the same thing can be achieved using Gluon.

First, let's define some constants that we'll use later to build, train, and test the MLP network:

```
nhn = 256 # number of hidden nodes for each layer
WeightScale = 0.01 # scale multiplier for weights
ModelCtx = mx.cpu() # assign context of the model itself
no = 3 # number of outputs (classes)
ne = 10 # number of epochs (for training)
lr = 0.001 # learning rate (for training)
sc = 0.01 # smoothing constant (for training)
ns = test.shape[0] # number of samples (for testing)
```

Next, let's initialize the network's parameters (weights and biases) for the first layer:

```
W1 = nd.random_normal(shape=(nf, nhn), scale=WeightScale,
    ctx=ModelCtx)
b1 = nd.random_normal(shape=nhn, scale=WeightScale, ctx=ModelCtx)
```

And do the same for the second layer:

```
W2 = nd.random_normal(shape=(nhn, nhn), scale=WeightScale,
    ctx=ModelCtx)
b2 = nd.random_normal(shape=nhn, scale=WeightScale, ctx=ModelCtx)
```

Then let's initialize the output layer and aggregate all the parameters into a single data structure called *params*:

```
W3 = nd.random_normal(shape=(nhn, no), scale=WeightScale,
    ctx=ModelCtx)
b3 = nd.random_normal(shape=no, scale=WeightScale, ctx=ModelCtx)
params = [W1, b1, W2, b2, W3, b3]
```

Finally, let's allocate some space for a gradient for each one of these parameters:

```
for param in params:
    param.attach_grad()
```

Remember that without any non-linear functions in the MLP's neurons, the whole system would be too rudimentary to be useful. We'll make use of the *ReLU* and the *Softmax* functions as activation functions for our system:

```
def relu(X): return nd.maximum(X, nd.zeros_like(X))
def softmax(y_linear):
    exp = nd.exp(y_linear - nd.max(y_linear))
    partition = nd.nansum(exp, axis=0, exclude=True).reshape((-1,
    1))
    return exp / partition
```

Note that the Softmax function will be used in the output neurons, while the ReLU function will be used in all the remaining neurons of the network.

For the cost function of the network (or, in other words, the fitness function of the optimization method under the hood), we'll use the cross-entropy function:

```
def cross_entropy(yhat, y): return - nd.nansum(y *
nd.log(yhat), axis=0, exclude=True)
```

To make the whole system a bit more efficient, we can combine the softmax and the cross-entropy functions into one, as follows:

```
def softmax_cross_entropy(yhat_linear, y):
```

```
return - nd.nansum(y * nd.log_softmax(yhat_linear), axis=0,
    exclude=True)
```

After all this, we can now define the function of the whole neural network, based on the above architecture:

```
def net(X):
    h1_linear = nd.dot(X, W1) + b1
    h1 = relu(h1_linear)
    h2_linear = nd.dot(h1, W2) + b2
    h2 = relu(h2_linear)
    yhat_linear = nd.dot(h2, W3) + b3
    return yhat_linear
```

The optimization method for training the system must also be defined. In this case we'll utilize a form of Gradient Descent:

```
def SGD(params, lr):
for param in params:
        param[:] = param - lr * param.grad
return param
```

For the purposes of this example, we'll use a simple evaluation metric for the model: accuracy rate. Of course, this needs to be defined first:

```
def evaluate_accuracy(data_iterator, net):
    numerator = 0.
    denominator = 0.
    for i, (data, label) in enumerate(data_iterator):
        data = data.as_in_context(model_ctx).reshape((-1, 784))
        label = label.as_in_context(model_ctx)
        output = net(data)
        predictions = nd.argmax(output, axis=1)
        numerator += nd.sum(predictions == label)
        denominator += data.shape[0]
    return (numerator / denominator).asscalar()
```

Now we can train the system as follows:

```
for e in range(epochs):
```

```
cumulative_loss = 0
for i, (data, label) in enumerate(train_data):
    data = data.as_in_context(model_ctx).reshape((-1, 784))
    label = label.as_in_context(model_ctx)
    label_one_hot = nd.one_hot(label, 10)
    with autograd.record():
        output = net(data)
        loss = softmax_cross_entropy(output, label_one_hot)
    loss.backward()
    SGD(params, learning_rate)
    cumulative_loss += nd.sum(loss).asscalar()
test_accuracy = evaluate_accuracy(test_data, net)
train_accuracy = evaluate_accuracy(train_data, net)
print("Epoch %s. Loss: %s, Train_acc %s, Test_acc %s" %
    (e, cumulative_loss/num_examples, train_accuracy,
 test_accuracy))
```

Finally, we can use to system to make some predictions using the following code:

```
def model_predict(net, data):
output = net(data)
return nd.argmax(output, axis=1)
SampleData = mx.gluon.data.DataLoader(data_test, ns,
    shuffle=True)
for i, (data, label) in enumerate(SampleData):
data = data.as_in_context(ModelCtx)
im = nd.transpose(data,(1,0,2,3))
im = nd.reshape(im,(28,10*28,1))
imtiles = nd.tile(im, (1,1,3))
plt.imshow(imtiles.asnumpy())
plt.show()
pred=model_predict(net,data.reshape((-1,784)))
print('model predictions are:', pred)
print('true labels :', label)
break
```

If you run the above code (preferably in the Docker environment provided), you will see that this simple MLP system does a good job at predicting the classes of some unknown data points—even if the class boundaries are highly non-linear.

Experiment with this system more and see how you can improve its performance even further, using the MXNet framework.

Now we'll see how we can significantly simplify all this by employing the Gluon interface. First, let's define a Python class to cover some common cases of Multi-Layer Perceptrons, transforming a "gluon.Block" object into something that can be leveraged to gradually build a neural network, consisting of multiple layers (also known as MLP):

```
class MLP(gluon.Block):
def __init__(self, **kwargs):
super(MLP, self).__init__(**kwargs)
    with self.name_scope():
    self.dense0 = gluon.nn.Dense(64) # architecture of 1st layer
    (hidden)
    self.dense1 = gluon.nn.Dense(64) # architecture of 2nd layer
    (hidden)
    self.dense2 = gluon.nn.Dense(3) # architecture of 3rd layer
    (output)
    def forward(self, x): # a function enabling an MLP to
    process data (x)                                              by
    passing it forward (towards the output layer)
        x = nd.relu(self.dense0(x)) # outputs of first hidden
    layer
        x = nd.relu(self.dense1(x)) # outputs of second hidden
    layer
        x = self.dense2(x) # outputs of final layer (output)
        return x
```

Of course, this is just an example of how you can define an MLP using Gluon, not a one-size-fits-all kind of solution. You may want to define the MLP class differently, since the architecture you use will have an impact on the system's performance. (This is particularly true for complex problems where additional hidden layers would be useful.) However, if you find what follows too challenging, and you don't have the time to assimilate the theory behind DL systems covered in Chapter 1, you can use an MLP object like the one above for your project.

Since DL systems are rarely as compact as the MLP above, and since we often need to add more layers (which would be cumbersome in the above approach), it is common to use a different class called *Sequential*. After we define the number of neurons in each hidden layer, and specify the activation function for these neurons, we can build an MLP like a ladder, with each step representing one layer in the MLP:

```
nhn = 64 # number of hidden neurons (in each layer)
af = "relu" # activation function to be used in each neuron
net = gluon.nn.Sequential()
with net.name_scope():
net.add(gluon.nn.Dense(nhn , activation=af))
net.add(gluon.nn.Dense(nhn , activation=af))
net.add(gluon.nn.Dense(no))
```

This takes care of the architecture for us. To make the above network functional, we'll first need to initialize it:

```
sigma = 0.1 # sigma value for distribution of weights for the ANN
    connections
ModelCtx = mx.cpu()
lr = 0.01 # learning rate
oa = 'sgd' # optimization algorithm
net.collect_params().initialize(mx.init.Normal(sigma=sigma),
    ctx=ModelCtx)
softmax_cross_entropy = gluon.loss.SoftmaxCrossEntropyLoss()
trainer = gluon.Trainer(net.collect_params(), oa,
    {'learning_rate': lr})
ne = 10 # number of epochs for training
```

Next, we must define how we assess the network's progress, through an evaluation metric function. For the purposes of simplicity, we'll use the standard accuracy rate metric:

```
def AccuracyEvaluation(iterator, net):
    acc = mx.metric.Accuracy()
    for i, (data, label) in enumerate(iterator):
        data = data.as_in_context(ModelCtx).reshape((-1, 3))
```

```
        label = label.as_in_context(ModelCtx)
        output = net(data)
        predictions = nd.argmax(output, axis=1)
        acc.update(preds=predictions, labels=label)
    return acc.get()[1]
```

Finally, it's time to train and test the MLP, using the aforementioned settings:

```
for e in range(ne):
    cumulative_loss = 0
    for i, (data, label) in enumerate(train_data):
        data = data.as_in_context(ModelCtx).reshape((-1, 784))
        label = label.as_in_context(ModelCtx)
        with autograd.record():
            output = net(data)
            loss = softmax_cross_entropy(output, label)
        loss.backward()
        trainer.step(data.shape[0])
        cumulative_loss += nd.sum(loss).asscalar()
    train_accuracy = AccuracyEvaluation(train_data, net)
    test_accuracy = AccuracyEvaluation(test_data, net)
    print("Epoch %s. Loss: %s, Train_acc %s, Test_acc %s" %
            (e, cumulative_loss/ns, train_accuracy, test_accuracy))
```

Running the above code should yield similar results to those from conventional mxnet commands.

To make things easier, we'll rely on the Gluon interface in the example that follows. Nevertheless, we still recommend that you experiment with the standard mxnet functions afterwards, should you wish to develop your own architectures (or better understand the theory behind DL).

Regression

Creating a regression MLP system is similar to creating a classification one but with some differences. In the regression case, the regression will be simpler, since regressors are typically lighter architecturally than classifiers. For this example, we'll use the second dataset.

First, let's start by importing the necessary classes from the mxnet package and setting the context for the model:

```
import mxnet as mx
from mxnet import nd, autograd, gluon
ModelCtx = mx.cpu()
```

To load data to the model, we'll use the dataloaders created previously (data_train2 and data_test2). Let's now define some basic settings and build the DL network gradually:

```
nf = 20 # we have 20 features in this dataset
sigma = 1.0 # sigma value for distribution of weights for the ANN
        connections
net = gluon.nn.Dense(1, in_units=nf) # the "1" here is the number
        of output
                neurons, which is 1 in regression
```

Let's now initialize the network with some random values for the weights and biases:

```
net.collect_params().initialize(mx.init.Normal(sigma=sigma),
        ctx=ModelCtx)
```

Just like any other DL system, we need to define the loss function. Using this function, the system understands how much of an error each deviation from the target variable's values costs. At the same time, cost functions can also deal with the complexity of the models (since if models are too complex they can cost us overfitting):

```
square_loss = gluon.loss.L2Loss()
```

Now it's time to train the network using the data at hand. After we define some essential parameters (just like in the classification case), we can create a loop for the network to train:

```
ne = 10 # number of epochs for training
loss_sequence = [] # cumulative loss for the various epochs
nb = ns / BatchSize # number of batches
for e in range(ne):
    cumulative_loss = 0
    for i, (data, label) in enumerate(train_data): # inner loop
        data = data.as_in_context(ModelCtx)
        label = label.as_in_context(ModelCtx)
        with autograd.record():
            output = net(data)
            loss = square_loss(output, label)
        loss.backward()
        trainer.step(BatchSize)
        CumulativeLoss += nd.mean(loss).asscalar()
    print("Epoch %s, loss: %s" % (e, CumulativeLoss / ns))
    loss_sequence.append(CumulativeLoss)
```

If you wish to view the parameters of the model, you can do so by collecting them into a dictionary structure:

```
params = net.collect_params()
for param in params.values():
print(param.name, param.data())
```

Printing out the parameters may not seem to be useful as we have usually too many of them and especially when we add new layers to the system, something we'd accomplish as follows:

```
net.add(gluon.nn.Dense(nhn))
```

where nhn is the number of neurons in that additional hidden layer. Note that the network requires an output layer with a single neuron, so be sure to insert any additional layers between the input and output layers.

Creating checkpoints for models developed in MXNet

As training a system may take some time, the ability to save and load DL models and data through this framework is essential. We must create "checkpoints" in our work so that we can pick up from where we've stopped, without having to recreate a network from scratch every time. This is achieved through the following process.

First import all the necessary packages and classes, and then define the context parameter:

```
import mxnet as mx
from mxnet import nd, autograd, gluon
import os
ctx = mx.cpu() # context for NDArrays
```

We'll then save the data, but let's put some of it into a dictionary first:

```
dict = {"X": X, "Y": Y}
```

Now we'll set the name of the file and save it:

```
filename = "test.dat"
nd.save(filename, dict)
```

We can verify that everything has been saved properly by loading that checkpoint as follows:

```
Z = nd.load(filename)
print(Z)
```

When using gluon, there is a shortcut for saving all the parameters of the DL network we have developed. It involves the *save_params()* function:

```
filename = "MyNet.params"
net.save_params(filename)
```

To restore the DL network, however, you'll need to recreate the original network's architecture, and then load the original network's parameters from the corresponding file:

```
net2 = gluon.nn.Sequential()with net2.name_scope():
    net2.add(gluon.nn.Dense(num_hidden, activation="relu"))
    net2.add(gluon.nn.Dense(num_hidden, activation="relu"))
    net2.add(gluon.nn.Dense(num_outputs))
net2.load_params(filename, ctx=ctx)
```

It's best to save your work at different parts of the pipeline, and give the checkpoint files descriptive names. It is also important to keep in mind that we don't have "untraining" option and it is likely that the optimal performance happens before the completion of the training phase. Because of this, we may want to create checkpoints after each training epoch so that we can revert to it when we find out at which point the optimal performance is achieved.

Moreover, for the computer to make sense of these files when you load them in your programming environment, you'll need to have the *nd* class of mxnet in memory, in whatever programming language you are using.

MXNet tips

The MXNet framework is a very robust and versatile platform for a variety of DL systems. Although we demonstrated its functionality in Python, it is equally powerful when used with other programming languages.

In addition, the Gluon interface is a useful add-on. If you are new to DL applications, we recommend you use Gluon as your go-to tool when employing the MXNet framework. This doesn't mean that the framework itself is limited to

Gluon, though, since the mxnet package is versatile and robust in a variety of programming platforms.

Moreover, in this chapter we covered just the basics of MXNet and Gluon. Going through all the details of these robust systems would take a whole book! Learn more about the details of the Gluon interface in the *Straight Dope* tutorial, which is part of the MXNet documentation.[9]

Finally, the examples in this chapter are executed in a Docker container; as such, you may experience some lagging. When developing a DL system on a computer cluster, of course, it is significantly faster.

Summary

- MXNet is a deep learning framework developed by Apache. It exhibits ease of use, flexibility, and high speed, among other perks. All of this makes MXNet an attractive option for DL, in a variety of programming languages, including Python, Julia, Scala, and R.

- MXNet models can be deployed to all kinds of computing systems, including smart devices. This is achieved by exporting them as a single file, to be executed by these devices.

- Gluon is a package that provides a simple interface for all your DL work using MXNet. Its main benefits include ease of use, no significant overhead, ability to handle dynamic graphs for your ANN models, and flexibility.

---

[9] http://gluon.mxnet.io/index.html.

- NDArrays are useful data structures when working with the MXNet framework. They can be imported as modules from the mxnet package as *nd*. They are similar to NumPy arrays, but more versatile and efficient when it comes to DL applications.

- The *mxnet* package is Python's API for the MXNet framework and contains a variety of modules for building and using DL systems.

- Data can be loaded into MXNet through an NDArray, directly from the data file; and then creating a *dataloader* object, to feed the data into the model built afterward.

- Classification in MXNet involves creating an MLP (or some other DL network), training it, and using it to predict unknown data, allocating one neuron for every class in the dataset. Classification is significantly simpler when using Gluon.

- Regression in MXNet is like classification, but the output layer has a single neuron. Also, additional care must be taken so that the system doesn't overfit; therefore we often use some regularization function such as L2.

- Creating project checkpoints in MXNet involves saving the model and any other relevant data into NDArrays, so that you can retrieve them at another time. This is also useful for sharing your work with others, for reviewing purposes.

- Remember that MXNet it is generally faster than on the Docker container used in this chapter's examples, and that it is equally useful and robust in other programming languages.

CHAPTER 4

Building a DL Network Using TensorFlow

This chapter provides an introduction to the most popular programming framework in the deep learning community: TensorFlow. Developed and backed by Google, TensorFlow has been adapted and advanced by a huge open source community. It is therefore essential for the deep learning practitioners to at least master the basics. In fact, much of the codes that you can find on the Internet are written in TensorFlow.

We'll cover the ingredients of the TensorFlow core library as well as some high-level APIs that are available in the Python ecosystem. Our discussion in this chapter should help you understand the basic structures of the framework, allowing you to build your own DL models using TensorFlow. Although we recommend using Keras (which we cover in the next chapter) if you are new to DL, learning the essentials of TensorFlow is quite useful, as Keras is also built on top of TensorFlow.[10]

TensorFlow is available both for Python 2 and Python 3. Since we're using Python 3 in this book, we briefly cover how to install TensorFlow on your local computer. However, if you're using the Docker file provided, TensorFlow is already installed for you.

---

[10] You can also use Keras on top of Theano or CNTK, but using it on top of TensorFlow is by far the most common usage in the industry.

Before installing TensorFlow, it is important to make note of the computation units on your machine that can be used by TensorFlow. You have two options to run your TensorFlow code: you can use the CPU or the GPU. Since GPUs are designed to run linear matrix operations faster than the CPUs, data scientists prefer to use GPUs when available. However, the TensorFlow code you write will be the same (except for the statement of your preference regarding the computation units you would like to use).

Let's start with the installation of the TensorFlow. In doing so, we make use of the pip package manager of Python. So, if Python 3 is the only installed version of Python in your machine, then the:

```
pip install -upgrade tensorflow
```

command would install Tensorflow for Python 3. However, if both Python 2 and Python 3 are installed in your computer, then the command above might install the TensorFlow for Python 2. In that case, you can also use the following command to install TensorFlow for Python 3:

```
pip3 install -upgrade tensorflow
```

The TensorFlow framework is now installed for you to explore. In your code, import the TensorFlow to use it:

```
import tensorflow
```

If you wish, you can rename it to "tf". We will do this throughout the chapter because it is the convention in the community:

```
import tensorflow as tf
```

TensorFlow architecture

The basic architecture of TensorFlow is shown in Figure 3. TensorFlow is designed as a distributed system by nature, so it is quite easy to run TensorFlow models in distributed settings. The TensorFlow Distributed Execution Engine is responsible for handling this capability of TensorFlow. As we mentioned before, TensorFlow models can be run on top of CPUs and GPUs. However, other computation units are also available to use. Recently, Google announced *Tensor Processing Units (TPUs)* that are designed to swiftly run TensorFlow models. You can even run TensorFlow in Android devices directly.

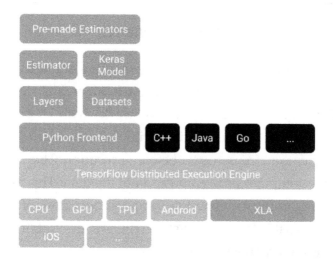

Figure 3: The architecture of TensorFlow. TensorFlow Distributed Execution Engine is what enables TensorFlow to run in a distributed environment. The several front ends include Python, Java, and Go. The Layers module includes different types of neural network modules, including a convolutional layer. The Datasets module includes utilities to work with external data. The Estimator and Keras are high level APIs on top of TensorFlow, which simplifies coding. TensorFlow is also bundled with several pre-built models. TensorFlow can run on CPU, GPU, TPU and Android devices. Source: https://bit.ly/2lwaybN.

Although Python is the most commonly used language with TensorFlow, you can use TensorFlow with C++, Java, Julia, Go, R, and more. TensorFlow includes two relatively high-level abstraction modules called *layers* and *datasets*. The

Layers module provides methods that simplify the creation of fully connected layers, convolutional layers, pooling layers, and more. It also provides methods like adding activation functions or applying dropout regularization. The Datasets module includes capabilities to manage your datasets.

Higher-level APIs (like Keras or Estimators) are easier to use, and they provide the same functionality of these lower-level modules. Lastly, we should mention that TensorFlow includes some pre-trained models out of the box.

Core components

To understand the core architecture of the TensorFlow framework, we introduce some basic concepts. First, let's begin with a fundamental design principle of TensorFlow: TensorFlow is designed to work with "static graphs". The computational flow of your model will be converted to a graphical representation in the framework before execution. The static graph in TensorFlow is the computational graph and not the data. This means that before you run the code, you must define the computational flow of your data. After that, all of the data that is fed to the system will flow through this computational graph, even if the data changes from time to time.

Let's start with the basic concepts of the framework. The first concept you have to understand is the "tensor" which is also included in the name of the framework. Tensors are the units that hold the data. You can think of tensors as NumPy n-dimensional arrays. The rank of the tensor defines the dimension, and the shape defines the lengths of each dimension in a tuple form. So

```
[ [1.0, 2.0, 3.0], [4.0, 5.0, 6.0] ]
```

is a tensor that has rank 2 and shape (2,3).

Another crucial concept of TensorFlow is the "directed graph", which contains operations and tensors. In this graph, operations are represented as nodes; tensors are represented as edges. Operations take tensors as input and produces tensors as output. Let's give a simple example here:

```
# first, we have to import tensorflow
Import tensorflow as tf
# constants are the most basic type of operations
x = tf.constant(1.0, dtype = tf.float32)
y = tf.constant(2.0, dtype = tf.float32)
z = x + y
```

In the code above, we define two tensors x and y by the tf.constant operation. This operation takes 1.0 and 2.0 as inputs and just produces their tensor equivalents and nothing more. Then using x and y, we created another tensor called z. Now, what do you expect from this code below?

```
print(z)
```

You are incorrect if you expect to see 3.0. Instead, you just see:

```
Tensor("add:0", shape=(), dtype=float32)
```

Defining graphs is different than executing the statements. For now, z is just a tensor object and has no value associated to it. We somehow need to run the graph so that we can get 3.0 from the tensor z. This is where another concept in the TensorFlow comes in: the *session*.

Sessions in TensorFlow are the objects that hold the state of the runtime where our graph will be executed. We need to instantiate a session and then run the operations we have already defined:

```
sess = tf.Session()
```

The code above instantiates the session object. Now, using that object, we can run our operations:

```
print(sess.run(z))
```

and we get 3.0 from the print statement! When we run an operation (namely a node in the graph), the TensorFlow executes it by calculating the tensors that our operation takes as input. This involves a backward calculation of the nodes and tensors, until it reaches a natural starting point – just like in our tf.constant operations above.

As you have already noticed, tf.constant simply provides constants as an operation; it may not be suitable to work with external data. For these kinds of situations, TensorFlow provides another object called the *placeholder*. You can think of placeholders as arguments to a function. It is something that you'll provide later on in your code! For example:

```
k = tf.placeholder(tf.float32)
l = tf.placeholder(tf.float32)
m = k + l
```

This time we define k and l as placeholders; we will assign some values to them when we run them in the session. Using the session above:

```
print(sess.run(m, feed_dict={k = 1.0, l = 2.0}))
```

will print 3.0. Here we used feed_dict object, which is a dictionary used to pass values to the placeholders. Effectively, we pass 1.0 and 2.0 to k and l placeholders, respectively, in the runtime. You can also use the feed_dict parameter of the run method of session to update values of the tf.constants.

We have seen that constants and placeholders are useful TensorFlow constructs to store values. Another useful construct is the TensorFlow *variable*. One can think of a variable as something that lies between constants and placeholders. Like placeholders, variables do not have an assigned value. However, much like constants, they can have default values. Here is an example of a TensorFlow variable:

```
v=  tf.Variable([0], tf.float32)
```

In the above line, we define a TensorFlow variable called v and set its default value as 0. When we want to assign some value different than the default one, we can use the tf.assign method:

```
w=  tf.assign(v, [-1.])
```

It is crucial to know that TensorFlow variables are not initialized when defined. Instead, we need to initialize them in the session like this:

```
init = tf.global_variables_initializer()
sess.run(init)
```

The code above initializes all the variables! As a rule of thumb, you should use tf.constant to define constants, tf.placeholder to hold the data fed to your model, and tf.Variable to represent the parameters for your model.

Now that we have learned the basic concepts of TensorFlow and demonstrated how to use them, you are all set to use TensorFlow to build your own models.

TensorFlow in action

We'll begin our TensorFlow exercises by implementing a DL classification model, utilizing the elements of TensorFlow we covered in the last section.

The datasets we use to demonstrate TensorFlow are the same synthetic datasets we used in the previous section. We use them for classification and regression purposes in this chapter. Remember that those datasets–as well as the codes we go over in this section–are already provided with the Docker image distributed with this book. You can run that Docker image to access the datasets and the source codes of this chapter.

Classification

Before we begin to implement our classifier, we need to import some libraries to use them. Here are the libraries we need to import:

```
import numpy as np
import pandas as pd
import tensorflow as tf
from sklearn.model_selection import train_test_split
```

First, we should load the dataset and do a bit of preprocessing to format the data we'll use in our model. As usual, we load the data as a list:

```
# import the data
with open("../data/data1.csv") as f:
    data_raw = f.read()
    # split the data into separate lines
    lines = data_raw.splitlines()
```

Then, we separate the labels and the three features into lists, called "labels" and "features":

```
labels = []
features = []
for line in lines:
    tokens = line.split(',')
    labels.append(int(tokens[-1]))
    x1,x2,x3 = float(tokens[0]), float(tokens[1]),
     float(tokens[2])
    features.append([x1, x2, x3])
```

Next, we make dummy variables of the three label categories, using Pandas' get_dummies function:

```
labels = pd.get_dummies(pd.Series(labels))
```

After this, the labels list should look like this:

	1	2	3
0	1	0	0
1	1	0	0
2	1	0	0

The next step is to split our data into train and test sets. For this purpose, we use the scikit-learn's train_test_split function that we imported before:

```
X_train, X_test, y_train, y_test = train_test_split(features, \
    labels, test_size=0.2, random_state=42)
```

We're now ready to build up our model using TensorFlow. First, we define the hyperparameters of the model that are related with the optimization process:

```
# Parameters
learning_rate = 0.1
epoch = 10
```

Next, we define the hyperparameters that are related with the structure of the model:

```
# Network Parameters
n_hidden_1 = 16 # 1st layer number of neurons
n_hidden_2 = 16 # 2nd layer number of neurons
num_input = 3 # data input
num_classes = 3 # total classes
```

Then we need the placeholders to store our data:

```
# tf Graph input
X = tf.placeholder("float", [None, num_input])
Y = tf.placeholder("float", [None, num_classes])
```

We will store the model parameters in two dictionaries:

```
# weights and biases
```

```
weights = {
    'h1': tf.Variable(tf.random_normal([num_input,n_hidden_1])),
    'h2': tf.Variable(tf.random_normal([n_hidden_1,n_hidden_2])),

    'out': tf.Variable(tf.random_normal([n_hidden_2, \
        num_classes]))
}
biases = {
    'b1': tf.Variable(tf.random_normal([n_hidden_1])),
    'b2': tf.Variable(tf.random_normal([n_hidden_2])),
    'out': tf.Variable(tf.random_normal([num_classes]))
}
```

We can now define our graph in TensorFlow. To that end, we provide a function:

```
# Create model
def neural_net(x):
    # Hidden fully connected layer with 16 neurons
    layer_1 = tf.nn.relu(tf.add(tf.matmul(x, weights['h1']), \
    biases['b1']))
    # Hidden fully connected layer with 16 neurons
    layer_2 = tf.nn.relu(tf.add(tf.matmul(layer_1, \
    weights['h2']), biases['b2']))
    # Output fully connected layer with a neuron for each class
    out_layer = tf.add(tf.matmul(layer_2, weights['out']), \
    biases['out'])
    # For visualization in TensorBoard
    tf.summary.histogram('output_layer', out_layer)
    return out_layer
```

This function takes the input data as an argument. Using this data, it first constructs a hidden layer. In this layer, each input data point is multiplied by the weights of the first layer, and added to the bias terms. Using the output of this layer, the function constructs another hidden layer. Similarly, this second layer multiplies the output of the first layer with the weights of its own and adds the result to the bias term. Then the output of the second layer is fed into the last layer which is the output layer of the neural network. The output layer does the same thing as the previous layers. As a result, the function we define just returns the output of the last layer.

After this, we can define our loss function, optimization algorithm, and the metric we will use to evaluate our model:

```
# Construct model
logits = neural_net(X)

# Define loss and optimizer
loss_op = tf.losses.softmax_cross_entropy(logits=logits, \
 onehot_labels=Y)
# For visualization in TensorBoard
tf.summary.scalar('loss_value', loss_op)
optimizer = tf.train.AdamOptimizer(learning_rate=learning_rate)
train_op = optimizer.minimize(loss_op)

# Evaluate model with test logits
correct_pred = tf.equal(tf.argmax(logits, 1), tf.argmax(Y, 1))
accuracy = tf.reduce_mean(tf.cast(correct_pred, tf.float32))
# For visualization in TensorBoard
tf.summary.scalar('accuracy', accuracy)

#For TensorBoard
merged = tf.summary.merge_all()
train_writer = tf.summary.FileWriter("events")
# Initialize the variables (assign their default value)
init = tf.global_variables_initializer()
```

As our loss function, we use the cross-entropy loss with softmax. Apart from this, there are other loss functions that are pre-built in TensorFlow. Some of them are: softmax, tanh, log_softmax, and weighted_cross_entropy_with_logits.

Adam is one of the most commonly used optimization algorithms in the machine learning community. Some other optimizers available in TensorFlow are: GradientDescentOptimizer, AdadeltaOptimizer, AdagradOptimizer, MomentumOptimizer, FtrlOptimizer, and RMSPropOptimizer.

Accuracy is our evaluation metric, as usual.

Now it's time to train our model!

```python
with tf.Session() as sess:

    # Run the initializer
    sess.run(init)
    # For visualization of the graph in TensorBoard
    train_writer.add_graph(sess.graph)
    for step in range(0, epoch):
        # Run optimization
        sess.run(train_op, feed_dict={X: X_train, Y: y_train})
        # Calculate loss and accuracy
        summary, loss, acc = sess.run([merged, loss_op, \
            accuracy], feed_dict={X: X_train, Y: y_train})
        # Add summary events for TensorBoard
        train_writer.add_summary(summary,step)
        print("Step " + str(step) + ", Loss= " + \
                "{:.4f}".format(loss) + ", Training Accuracy= "+ \
                "{:.3f}".format(acc))

    print("Optimization Finished!")

    # Calculate test accuracy
    acc = sess.run(accuracy, feed_dict={X: X_test, Y: y_test})
    print("Testing Accuracy:", acc)

    # close the FileWriter
    train_writer.close()
```

After several iterations, you should see an output similar to this:

```
Step 0, Loss= 0.4989, Training Accuracy= 0.821
Step 1, Loss= 0.2737, Training Accuracy= 0.898
Step 2, Loss= 0.2913, Training Accuracy= 0.873
Step 3, Loss= 0.3024, Training Accuracy= 0.864
Step 4, Loss= 0.2313, Training Accuracy= 0.892
Step 5, Loss= 0.1640, Training Accuracy= 0.933
Step 6, Loss= 0.1607, Training Accuracy= 0.943
Step 7, Loss= 0.1684, Training Accuracy= 0.938
```

```
Step 8, Loss= 0.1537, Training Accuracy= 0.944
Step 9, Loss= 0.1242, Training Accuracy= 0.956
Optimization Finished!
Testing Accuracy: 0.95476
```

Regression

Although today's deep learning applications are quite successful in challenging classification tasks, TensorFlow also enables us to build regression models in almost the same manner. In this section, we'll show you how to predict a continuous outcome variable using regression.

It is critical to choose a different loss function than we used in the classification model – one that is more suitable to a regression task. We'll choose the L2 metric, as it is one of the most popular metrics in regression analysis. In terms of evaluation, we'll use R-squared to assess the performance of our model in the test set.

We import the same libraries that we imported for the classification task:

```
import numpy as np
import pandas as pd
import tensorflow as tf
from sklearn.model_selection import train_test_split
```

The dataset we use is the same synthetic set provided, with 20 features and 1 outcome variable. Below, we load the dataset and do some pre-processing to format the data we'll use in our model:

```
import the data
with open("../data/data2.csv") as f:
    data_raw = f.read()
    # split the data into separate lines
    lines = data_raw.splitlines()
```

Instead of calling the outcome variable as "labels", we prefer to call it "outcomes" in this case as this seems more appropriate for regression models. As usual, we separate 20% of our dataset as our test data.

```
outcomes = []
features = []
for line in lines:
    tokens = line.split(',')
    outcomes.append(float(tokens[-1]))
    features.append([float(x) for x in tokens[:-1]])

X_train, X_test, y_train, y_test = train_test_split(features, \
    outcomes, test_size=0.2, random_state=42)
```

We can now set the hyperparameters of the model regarding the optimization process, and define the structure of our model:

```
# Parameters
learning_rate = 0.1
epoch = 500

# Network Parameters
n_hidden_1 = 64 # 1st layer number of neurons
n_hidden_2 = 64 # 2nd layer number of neurons
num_input = 20 # data input
num_classes = 1 # total classes

# tf Graph input
X = tf.placeholder("float", [None, num_input])
Y = tf.placeholder("float", [None, num_classes])
```

This time, our outcome is single-value in nature, and we have 20 features. We set the relevant parameters accordingly, above. Next, we store the model parameters in two dictionaries as we did in the classification case:

```
# weights & biases
weights = {
    'h1': tf.Variable(tf.random_normal([num_input,n_hidden_1])),
    'h2': tf.Variable(tf.random_normal([n_hidden_1,n_hidden_2])),
```

```
    'out': tf.Variable(tf.random_normal([n_hidden_2, \
        num_classes]))
}
biases = {
    'b1': tf.Variable(tf.random_normal([n_hidden_1])),
    'b2': tf.Variable(tf.random_normal([n_hidden_2])),
    'out': tf.Variable(tf.random_normal([num_classes]))
}
```

It's time to define the structure of our model. The graph is exactly the same as the graph of the classification model we used in the previous part:

```
# Create model
def neural_net(x):
    # Hidden fully connected layer with 64 neurons
    layer_1 = tf.add(tf.matmul(x, weights['h1']), biases['b1'])
    # Hidden fully connected layer with 64 neurons
    layer_2 = tf.add(tf.matmul(layer_1, weights['h2']), \
     biases['b2'])
    # Output fully connected layer
    out_layer = tf.matmul(layer_2, weights['out']) \
    + biases['out']
    return out_layer
```

The difference between the classification model and the regression model is that the latter uses the L2 loss as a loss function. This is because the outcome of the regression model is continuous; as such, we must use a loss function that is capable of handling continues loss values. We also use the Adam optimization algorithm in this regression model.

```
# Construct model
output = neural_net(X)

# Define loss and optimizer
loss_op = tf.nn.l2_loss(tf.subtract(Y, output))
optimizer = tf.train.AdamOptimizer(learning_rate=learning_rate)
train_op = optimizer.minimize(loss_op)
```

Another difference between our classification and regression models is the metric we use to evaluate our model. For regression models, we prefer to use the R-squared metric; it is one of the most common metrics used to assess the performance of regression models:

```
# Evaluate model using R-squared

total_error = tf.reduce_sum(tf.square(tf.subtract(Y, \
    tf.reduce_mean(Y))))

unexplained_error = tf.reduce_sum(tf.square(tf.subtract(Y, \
    output)))

R_squared = tf.subtract(1.0,tf.div(unexplained_error, \
    total_error))

# Initialize the variables (assign their default values)
init = tf.global_variables_initializer()
```

We are all set to train our model:

```
# Start training
with tf.Session() as sess:

    # Run the initializer
    sess.run(init)

    for step in range(0, epoch):
        # Run optimization
        sess.run(train_op,feed_dict= \
            {X: X_train, \
             Y:np.array(y_train).reshape(200000,1)})

        # Calculate batch loss and accuracy
        loss, r_sq = sess.run([loss_op, R_squared], \
            feed_dict={X: X_train, \
                       Y: np.array(y_train).reshape(200000,1)})

        print("Step " + str(step) + ", L2 Loss= " + \
            "{:.4f}".format(loss) + ", Training R-squared= " \
```

```
        + "{:.3f}".format(r_sq))

print("Optimization Finished!")

# Calculate accuracy for MNIST test images
print("Testing R-squared:", \
    sess.run(R_squared, feed_dict={X: X_test, \
            Y: np.array(y_test).reshape(50000,1)}))
```

The outcome of the model should look like this:

```
Step 497, L2 Loss= 81350.7812, Training R-squared= 0.992
Step 498, L2 Loss= 81342.4219, Training R-squared= 0.992
Step 499, L2 Loss= 81334.3047, Training R-squared= 0.992
Optimization Finished!
Testing R-squared: 0.99210745
```

Visualization in TensorFlow: TensorBoard

Visualization of your model's results is useful method for investigation, understanding, and debugging purposes. To this end, TensorFlow offers a visualization library called TensorBoard; with that library, you can visualize your models and their outcomes. TensorBoard comes with TensorFlow; once you install TensorFlow on your machine, TensorBoard should be present.

TensorBoard reads event files containing the summary data of the TensorFlow model. To generate summary data, TensorFlow provides some functions in the summary module. In this module, there are some functions that operate just like the operations in TensorFlow. This means that we can use tensors and operations as input for these summary operations.

In the classification example, we actually used some of these functionalities. Here is a summary of the operations that we used in our example:

tf.summary.scalar: If we want data about how a scalar evolves in time (like our loss function), we can use the loss function node as an input for the tf.summary.scalar function—right after we define the loss, as shown in the following example:

```
loss_op = tf.reduce_mean(tf.nn.softmax_cross_entropy_with_logits(
logits=logits, labels=Y))
tf.summary.scalar('loss_value', loss_op)
```

tf.summary.histogram: We may also be interested in the distributions of some variables, like the results of a matrix multiplication. In this case we use tf.summary.histogram, as follows:

```
out_layer = tf.matmul(layer_2, weights['out']) + biases['out']
tf.summary.histogram('output_layer', out_layer)
```

tf.summary.merge_all: Summary nodes do not alter the graph of the model, but we need them to run our summary operations. The tf.summary.merge_all function merges all of our summary operations so that we do not need to run each operation one by one.

tf.summary.FileWriter: This function is used to store the summary (which was generated using the tf.summary.merge_all function) to the disk. Here is an example of how to do that:

```
merged = tf.summary.merge_all()
train_writer = tf.summary.FileWriter("events")
```

Once we define our file writers, we also need to initialize them inside the session:

```
train_writer.add_graph(sess.graph)
```

After we integrate summary functions to our code, we should write the summaries to the files and visualize them. When we run our model, we also receive the summaries:

```
summary, loss, acc = sess.run([merged, loss_op, accuracy],
    feed_dict={X: batch_x, Y: batch_y})
```

After that we add the summary to our summary file:

```
train_writer.add_summary(summary,step)
```

Last, we close the FileWriter:

```
train_writer.close()
```

Next, we can visualize the summaries in the browser. To do that, we need to run the following command:

```
tensorboard –logdir=path/to/log-directory
```

where the log-directory refers to the directory where we saved our summary files. When you open localhost:6006 in your browser, you should see the dashboard with the summaries of your model, similar to the one in Figure 4.

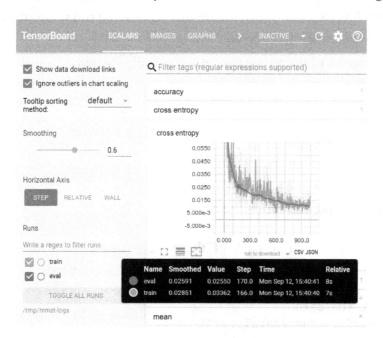

Figure 4: Dashboard of the TensorBoard. Source: https://bit.ly/2IWkbxh.

High level APIs in TensorFlow: Estimators

So far, we've discussed the low-level structures of TensorFlow. We saw that we must build our own graph and keep track of the session. However, TensorFlow also provides a high-level API, where the tedious works are handled automatically. This high-level API is called "Estimators".

Estimators API also provides pre-made estimators. You can use these estimators quickly, and customize them if needed. Here are some of the advantages of this API, with respect to the low-level APIs of TensorFlow:

- With fewer lines of codes, you can implement the same model.
- Building the graph, opening and closing the session, and initializing the variables are all handled automatically.
- The same code runs in CPU, GPU, or TPU.
- Parallel computing is supported. As such, if multiple servers are available, the code you write on this API can be run without any modification of the code you run on your local machine.
- Summaries of the models are automatically saved for TensorBoard.

When you are writing your code using this API, you basically follow four steps:

1. Reading the dataset.
2. Defining the feature columns.
3. Setting up a pre-defined estimator.
4. Training and evaluating the estimator.

Now we will demonstrate each of these steps using our synthetic data for classification. First, we read the data from our .csv file, as usual:

```
# import the data
with open("../data/data1.csv") as f:
    data_raw = f.read()
```

```
        lines = data_raw.splitlines() # split the data into separate
        lines
labels = []
x1 = []
x2 = []
x3 = []
for line in lines:
    tokens = line.split(',')
    labels.append(int(tokens[-1])-1)
    x1.append(float(tokens[0]))
    x2.append(float(tokens[1]))
    x3.append(float(tokens[2]))
features = np.array([x1,x2,x3]).reshape(250000,3)
labels = np.array(pd.Series(labels))

X_train, X_test, y_train, y_test = train_test_split(features,
    labels, test_size=0.2, random_state=42)
```

Second, we write a function that converts our features to a dictionary, and returns the features and labels for the model:

```
def inputs(features,labels):
    features = {'x1': features[:,0],
                'x2': features[:,1],
                'x3': features[:,2]}
    labels = labels
    return features, labels
```

Third, we write a function that transforms our data into a DataSet object:

```
def train_input_fn(features, labels, batch_size):
    # Convert the inputs to a Dataset.
    dataset = tf.data.Dataset.from_tensor_slices((dict(features),
     labels))
    # Shuffle, repeat, and batch the examples.
    return dataset.shuffle(1000).repeat().batch(batch_size)
```

Defining our feature columns only requires a few lines of code:

```
# Feature columns describe how to use the input.
my_feature_columns = []
```

```
for key in ['x1','x2','x3']:

    my_feature_columns.append(tf.feature_column.numeric_column(k
    ey=key))
```

Before we run our model, we should select a pre-defined estimator that is suitable for our needs. Since our task is classification, we use two fully-connected layers, as we did previously. For this, the estimator's API provides a classifier called *DNNClassifier*:

```
# Build a DNN with 2 hidden layers and 256 nodes in each hidden
    layer.
classifier = tf.estimator.DNNClassifier(
    feature_columns=my_feature_columns,
    # Two hidden layers of 256 nodes each.
    hidden_units=[256, 256],
    # The model must choose between 3 classes.
    n_classes=3,
    optimizer=tf.train.AdamOptimizer(
      learning_rate=0.1
    ))
```

As before, we defined two dense layers of size 256, we set the learning rate to 0.1, and we set the number of classes to 3.

Now, we are ready to train and evaluate our model. Training is as simple as:

```
classifier.train(input_fn=lambda:train_input_fn(inputs(X_train,y_
    train)[0], inputs(X_train,y_train)[1], 64), steps=500)
```

We provided the function that we wrote above, which returns the DataSet object for the model as an argument to the train() function. We also set training steps to 500, as usual. When you run the code above, you should see something like:

```
INFO:tensorflow:loss = 43.874107, step = 401 (0.232 sec)
INFO:tensorflow:Saving checkpoints for 500 into
    /tmp/tmp8xv6svzr/model.ckpt.
INFO:tensorflow:Loss for final step: 34.409817.
```

```
<tensorflow.python.estimator.canned.dnn.DNNClassifier at
    0x7ff14f59b2b0>
```

After this, we can evaluate the performance of our model in our test set:

```
# Evaluate the model.
eval_result = classifier.evaluate(
    input_fn=lambda:train_input_fn(inputs(X_test,y_test)[0],
    inputs(X_test,y_test)[1], 64), steps=1)
print('Test set accuracy:
    {accuracy:0.3f}\n'.format(**eval_result))
```

The output should look like this:

```
INFO:tensorflow:Starting evaluation at 2018-04-07-12:11:21
INFO:tensorflow:Restoring parameters from
    /tmp/tmp8xv6svzr/model.ckpt-500
INFO:tensorflow:Evaluation [1/1]
INFO:tensorflow:Finished evaluation at 2018-04-07-12:11:21
INFO:tensorflow:Saving dict for global step 500: accuracy =
    0.828125, average_loss = 0.6096449, global_step = 500, loss
    = 39.017273
Test set accuracy: 0.828
```

Summary

- TensorFlow is a deep learning framework initially developed by Google and now backed by a huge open source community.

- TensorFlow is by far the most popular deep learning framework. Even if you choose to use other frameworks, learning the basics of TensorFlow is beneficial; many of the codes you'll encounter that are written by others will likely be written in TensorFlow.

- TensorFlow supports distributed computing by nature.

- TensorFlow models can be run on CPUs, GPUs, and TPUs.

- You can write TensorFlow code in Python, Java, Julia, C++, R, and more.

- Although you can use low-level structures of TensorFlow, there are also many high-level APIs that simplify the model building process.

## CHAPTER 5

Building a DL Network Using Keras

Now that you understand the basics of the TensorFlow framework, we'll explore another very popular framework that is built on top of TensorFlow: Keras. Keras is a framework that reduces the lines of code you need to write by means of its abstraction layers. It provides a simple yet powerful API that almost anyone can implement even a complicated DL models with just a few lines of code.

Our advice is to use Keras if you are new to DL, as you can implement almost anything just using Keras. Nevertheless, being familiar with TensorFlow is also beneficial. You'll likely encounter models that are written in TensorFlow, and to understand them you'll need a good grasp of TensorFlow. This is one of the reasons why we introduced TensorFlow before Keras. The other reason is that we can now appreciate the simplicity Keras brings to the table, compared to TensorFlow!

We cover the basic structures in Keras, and show how you can implement DL models in Keras using our synthetic dataset. Next, we explore the visualization capabilities of the framework. Then, we show you how to transform your models written in Keras into TensorFlow estimators.

Keras sits on top of a back-end engine which is either TensorFlow, Theano, or CNTK. So, before installing Keras, one should first install one of these three back ends that Keras supports. By default, Keras supports the TensorFlow back-end engine. Since we covered TensorFlow in the last chapter, we assume that you've already installed TensorFlow on your system. If not, refer to the relevant section of the TensorFlow chapter to install TensorFlow first.

After installing TensorFlow, Keras can be installed via PyPl.[11] Simply run this command:

```
pip install keras
```

After you run the command above, the Keras deep learning framework should be installed in your system. After importing it, you can use Keras in your Python code as follows:

```
import keras
```

Keras abstracts away the low-level data structures of TensorFlow, replacing them with intuitive, easily integrated, and extensible structures. When designing this framework, the developers followed these guiding principles:

1. **User friendliness**: Keras makes human attention focus on the model and builds up the details around this structure. In doing so, it reduces the amount of work done in common-use cases by providing relevant functionality by default.

2. **Modularity**: In Keras, we can easily integrate the layers, optimizers, activation layers, and other ingredients of a DL model together, as if they were modules.

---

[11] TensorFlow now integrates Keras in its core. So, no need to install Keras additionally if you already installed TensorFlow. However, we want to emphasize Keras as a separate framework as you might prefer to use it on top of Theano or CNTK. In this respect, we prefer to install Keras separately.

3. **Easy extensibility**: We can create new modules in Keras and integrate them to our existing models quite easily. They can be used as objects or functions.

Core components

The basic component in Keras is called the *model*. You can think of the Keras model as an abstraction of a deep learning model. When we start to implement a DL model in Keras, we usually begin by creating a so-called *model object*. Of the many types of models in Keras, Sequential is the simplest and the most commonly used.

Another basic structure in Keras is called the *layer*. Layer objects in Keras represent the actual layers in a DL model. We can add layer objects to our model object by just defining the type of the layer, the number of units, and the input/output sizes. The most commonly used layer type is the Dense layer.

And that is all! You might be surprised that the authors forgot to mention some other critical parts of the Keras framework. However, as you'll see below, you can now start to build up your model with what you've already learned so far!

Keras in action

Now it's time to see Keras in action. Remember that the datasets and the codes examined in this section are available to you via the Docker image provided with the book.

The datasets used to demonstrate Keras are the same synthetic datasets used in the chapter on TensorFlow. We'll again use them for classification and regression purposes.

Classification

Before we begin to implement our classifier, we need to import some libraries in order to use them. Here are the libraries we need to import:

```
import numpy as np
import pandas as pd
from keras.models import Sequential
from keras.layers import Dense
from keras import optimizers
from sklearn.model_selection import train_test_split
```

First, we should load the dataset, and do a bit of pre-processing to format the data we'll use in our model. As usual, we load the data as a list:

```
# import the data
with open("../data/data1.csv") as f:
            data_raw = f.read()
        lines = data_raw.splitlines() # split the data into
    separate lines
```

Then, we separate the labels and the three features into lists, respectively called labels and features:

```
labels = []
features = []
for line in lines:
                tokens = line.split(',')
                labels.append(int(tokens[-1]))
                x1,x2,x3 = float(tokens[0]), float(tokens[1]),
    float(tokens[2])
        features.append([x1, x2, x3])
```

Next, we make dummy variables of the three label categories using Pandas' get_dummies function:

```
labels = pd.get_dummies(pd.Series(labels))
```

The next step is to split our data into train and test sets. For this purpose, we use the scikit-learn's train_test_split function that we imported before:

```
X_train, X_test, y_train, y_test = train_test_split(features,
    labels, test_size=0.2, random_state=42)
```

We're now ready to build up our model using Keras. We first define our model and then add three layers; the first two are the dense layers and the third is the output layer:

```
model = Sequential()
model.add(Dense(units=16, activation='relu', input_dim=3))
model.add(Dense(units=16, activation='relu'))
model.add(Dense(units=3, activation='softmax'))
```

As you can see, building a graph in Keras is quite an easy task. In the code above, we first define a model object (which is sequential, in this case). Then we add three fully-connected layers (called *dense layers*).

After we define our model and layers, we must choose our optimizer and compile our model. For the optimizer, we use Adam, setting its learning rate to 0.1:

```
sgd = optimizers.Adam(lr=0.1)
```

Then we compile our model. In doing so, we define our loss function to be categorical cross-entropy, which is one of the pre-defined loss functions in Keras. For the metric to evaluate the performance of our model, we use accuracy, as usual. All these definitions can be implemented in a single line in Keras as seen here:

```
model.compile(loss='categorical_crossentropy', optimizer=sgd,
    metrics= ['accuracy'])
```

Now, it's time to train our model in a single line! We train our models by calling the fit function of the model object. As parameters, we provide our features and labels as NumPy arrays—the batch size and the epochs. We define the batch size as 10.000 and the epochs as 5:

```
model.fit(np.array(X_train), np.array(y_train), batch_size=10000,
    epochs = 5)
```

During the training you should see something like this in the console:

```
Epoch 1/5
200000/200000 [==============================] - 0s 2us/step -
    loss: 0.3671 - acc: 0.8255
Epoch 2/5
200000/200000 [==============================] - 0s 2us/step -
    loss: 0.0878 - acc: 0.9650
Epoch 3/5
200000/200000 [==============================] - 0s 2us/step -
    loss: 0.0511 - acc: 0.9790
Epoch 4/5
200000/200000 [==============================] - 0s 2us/step -
    loss: 0.0409 - acc: 0.9839
Epoch 5/5
200000/200000 [==============================] - 0s 2us/step -
    loss: 0.0368 - acc: 0.9854
```

Next, we evaluate the performance of the model in our test data:

```
loss_and_metrics = model.evaluate(np.array(X_test),
    np.array(y_test), batch_size=100)
print(loss_and_metrics)
```

It should print out:

```
[0.03417351390561089, 0.9865800099372863]
```

So our model's loss value is approximately 0.03 and the accuracy in the test set is about 0.99!

Regression

In Keras, building regression models is as simple as building classification models. We first define our models and the layers. One thing to be aware of is that the output layer of a regression model must produce only a single value.

We also must choose a different loss function. As we did in the TensorFlow chapter, we use the L2 metric, as it is one of the most popular metrics in regression analysis. Finally, we evaluate the performance of our model using R-squared.

Import the following libraries:

```
import numpy as np
import pandas as pd
from keras.models import Sequential
from keras.layers import Dense
from keras import optimizers
import keras.backend as K
from sklearn.model_selection import train_test_split
```

We'll again utilize the synthetic dataset from the previous chapter. Recall that it includes 20 features and 1 outcome variable. Below, we load the dataset and pre-process the data into the format we'll use in our model:

```
# import the data
with open("../data/data2.csv") as f:
    data_raw = f.read()
    lines = data_raw.splitlines() # split the data into separate
    lines
```

Instead of "label" we prefer to call the target variable "outcome," as it is more appropriate for regression models. As usual, we separate 20% of our dataset as our test data.

```
outcomes = []
features = []
for line in lines:
    tokens = line.split(',')
    outcomes.append(float(tokens[-1]))
        features.append([float(x) for x in tokens[:-1]])

X_train, X_test, y_train, y_test = train_test_split(features,
    outcomes, test_size=0.2, random_state=42)
```

We define our model and the layers as follows:

```
model = Sequential()
model.add(Dense(units=64, activation='relu', input_dim=20))
model.add(Dense(units=64, activation='relu'))
model.add(Dense(units=1, activation='linear'))
```

This time, our outcome is a single value and we have 20 features. So, we set the relevant parameters accordingly.

It's time to compile our model. First, though, we must define a function that calculates the R-squared metric. Unfortunately, as of this writing, Keras does not provide a built-in R-squared metric in its package. As such, consider our implementation:

```
def r2(y_true, y_pred):
    SS_res =  K.sum(K.square(y_true - y_pred))
    SS_tot = K.sum(K.square(y_true - K.mean(y_true)))
    return ( 1 - SS_res/(SS_tot + K.epsilon()) )
```

After that we choose Adam as our optimizer and set the learning rate to 0.1:

```
sgd = optimizers.Adam(lr=0.1)
```

Now we can compile our model. We use the mean-squared error as our loss function, and we feed our r2() function to the model as a metric:

```
model.compile(optimizer=sgd,
              loss='mean_squared_error',
              metrics=[r2])
```

Training a model is quite simple in Keras, as we saw earlier with classification. We provide our features and outcomes as NumPy arrays to the fit function of the model object. We also set the batch size to 10.000 and epochs to 10:

```
model.fit(np.array(X_train), np.array(y_train), batch_size=10000,
    epochs = 10)
```

The outcome of the model should look like this:

```
Epoch 1/10
200000/200000 [==============================] - 1s 5us/step -
    loss: 240.4952 - r2: -1.3662
Epoch 2/10
200000/200000 [==============================] - 0s 2us/step -
    loss: 83.3737 - r2: 0.1800
Epoch 3/10
200000/200000 [==============================] - 0s 2us/step -
    loss: 27.3745 - r2: 0.7308
Epoch 4/10
200000/200000 [==============================] - 0s 2us/step -
    loss: 5.7173 - r2: 0.9439
Epoch 5/10
200000/200000 [==============================] - 0s 2us/step -
    loss: 3.4069 - r2: 0.9665
Epoch 6/10
200000/200000 [==============================] - 0s 2us/step -
    loss: 3.0487 - r2: 0.9700
Epoch 7/10
200000/200000 [==============================] - 0s 2us/step -
    loss: 2.9293 - r2: 0.9712
Epoch 8/10
200000/200000 [==============================] - 0s 2us/step -
    loss: 2.8396 - r2: 0.9721
```

```
Epoch 9/10
200000/200000 [==============================] - 0s 2us/step -
    loss: 2.7537 - r2: 0.9729
Epoch 10/10
200000/200000 [==============================] - 0s 2us/step -
    loss: 2.6688 - r2: 0.9738
```

Next we evaluate the performance of our model on the test data:

```
loss_and_metrics = model.evaluate(np.array(X_test),
    np.array(y_test), batch_size=100)
print(loss_and_metrics)
```

The output should be similar to this:

```
50000/50000 [==============================] - 0s 7us/step
[2.6564363064765932, 0.9742180906534195]
```

So our model achieves 0.97 R-squared in the test data.

Model Summary and Visualization

If you don't need any visuals, Keras can easily provide a textual summary of the layers of the model. For this purpose, Keras provides a summary() function. When called from a model, it returns the textual information about the model. By just printing the summary of a model using the code below, it is possible to check out the structure of the model:

```
print(model.summary())
```

Depending on the structure of the model, the output should look something like this:

Layer (type)	Output Shape	Param #
dense_1 (Dense)	(None, 2)	4
dense_2 (Dense)	(None, 1)	3

Total params: 7
Trainable params: 7
Non-trainable params: 0

Of course, visualizations are not only more aesthetically pleasing, but also can help you easily explain and share your findings with stakeholders and team members. Graphically visualizing the model in Keras is straightforward. A module named keras.utils.vis_utils includes all the utilities for visualizing the graph using a library called graphviz. Specifically, the plot_model() function is the basic tool for visualizing the model. The code below demonstrates how to create and save the graph visualization for a model:

```
from keras.utils import plot_model
plot_model(model, to_file = "my_model.png")
```

Depending on the structure of the model, the png file should contain a graph like the one in Figure 5:

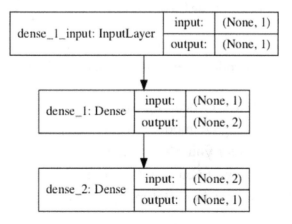

Figure 5: A visualization of the model graph in Keras.

The plot_model() function accepts two optional arguments:

- show_shapes: if True the graph shows the output shapes. The default setting is False.
- show_layer_names: if True the graph shows the names of the layers. The default setting is True.

Converting Keras models to TensorFlow Estimators

As we mentioned in the previous chapter, TensorFlow provides a rich set of pre-trained models that you can use without any training. The Estimators abstraction of TensorFlow will allow you to use these pre-trained models. To make full use of this rich set of models, it would be nice to convert our Keras models into TensorFlow Estimators. Thankfully, Keras provides this functionality out of the box. With just a single line of code, Keras models turn into TensorFlow Estimators, ready to be used. The function is called model_to_estimator() in the keras.estimator module, and looks like this:

```
estimator_model =
keras.estimator.model_to_estimator(keras_model = model)
```

Once we convert our Keras model into TensorFlow Estimator, we can use this estimator in TensorFlow code (as we demonstrated in the previous chapter).

Before closing the chapter, we encourage our users to read more about the Keras framework. If you are using DL models for research purposes, Keras is probably the most convenient tool for you. Keras will save a lot of time in implementing the many models you'll try. If you're a data science practitioner, Keras is one of the best choices for you both in prototyping and production. Hence, enhancing your understanding and expertise in Keras is beneficial regardless of your particular problem.

Summary

- Keras is a deep learning framework that provides a convenient and easy-to-use abstraction layer on top of the TensorFlow framework.

- Keras brings a more user-friendly API to the TensorFlow framework. Along with easy extensibility and modularity, these are the key advantages of Keras over other frameworks.

- The main structure in Keras is the model object, which represents the deep learning model to be used. The most commonly-used model type is the sequential model. Another important structure in Keras is the layer, which represents the layers in the model; the most common layer is the Dense layer.

- Visualizing the model structure in Keras is accomplished with a single function call to plot_model().

- It is a good idea to start building deep learning models in Keras instead of TensorFlow if you are new to the field.

- Although Keras provides a very wide range of functionality, one may need to switch to TensorFlow to write some sophisticated functionality for non-standard deep learning models.

## CHAPTER 6

Building an Optimizer Based on the Particle Swarm Optimization Algorithm

We'll start our examination of optimization frameworks with one of the most powerful and easy-to-use optimizers, known as Particle Swarm Optimization (or PSO). This optimizer was named after the biological phenomenon of a "swarm," say of bees or of starlings. In such swarms, large groups of individuals behave in a cooperative manner, more like one large organism than the sum of its parts. The name fits because the optimizer mimics the swarm movement in an attempt to solve the complex optimization problems it is designed for. In fact, many of the other optimizers we'll discuss later in the book are similarly named after such types of natural phenomena.

The significance of PSO lies in the fact that many of the alternative optimizers are merely variations of the cornerstone PSO. As a result, understanding this optimizer grants you access to a whole set of optimization methods that can solve much more than conventional data analytics problems. In fact, their applications span over so many fields that one can argue that many data analytics methods are just a niche application of this AI framework.

PSO belongs to a general class of systems called Evolutionary Computation, which is a type of *Computational Intelligence*. Computational Intelligence is a popular subclass of AI (at least in the research world) that involves the development and application of clever ways to solve complex problems, using just a computational approach.

In this chapter, we'll examine the inner workings of PSO, as well as some of its most important variants, with a focus on the Firefly optimizer. We'll also show how PSO can be implemented in Julia. We'll close with some useful considerations about PSO, and a summary of the key points of this chapter.

PSO algorithm

The logic behind PSO is to have a set of potential solutions (akin to a swarm of particles) that continuously evolve, becoming better and better, based on some fitness function the system tries to maximize or minimize. The particles "move" with varying speeds throughout several dimensions (also called variables), influenced by the best-performing particle, so that they collectively reach an optimal solution in an efficient manner.

In addition, each particle "remembers" its best performance historically, and it takes that into account when changing its position. Naturally, the best performing particle may be a different one over the duration of the search (you can imagine the group of solutions moving towards the best possible solution like a swarm of insects, so which insect is closest to that solution is bound to be different every time you look at the swarm). Still, there is generally an improvement in the best solution over time, even if the rate of this improvement gradually diminishes. This is because the closer you get to the best solution, the more likely the swarm is bound to deviate from it (albeit slightly) while "zeroing in" on that best solution.

All these traits make the PSO algorithm ideal for optimizing the parameters of a complex system. PSO is relatively new as an algorithm; its creators, Dr. Eberhart and Dr. Kennedy, invented it in 1995. The pseudocode of PSO is as follows:

```
For each particle in the swarm
    Initialize particle by setting random values to its initial
    state
End
Do
    For each particle in the swarm
        Calculate fitness value
        If the fitness value is better than the best fitness
    value in its history (pBest): pBest <-- fitness value of
    particle
    End
gBest <-- particle with the best fitness value of all the
    particles in the swarm
    For each particle
        Calculate particle velocity according to equation A
        Update particle position according to equation B
    End
Repeat Until maximum iterations is reached OR minimum error
    criteria is attained
```

The key equations for the updating of a particle's speed and position, respectively, are the following:

```
eq. A: v[] += c₁ * rand() * (pbest[] - present[]) + c₂ * rand() *
    (gbest[] - present[])
eq. B: present[] += v[]
```

Note that c_1 and c_2 are parameters of the PSO algorithm, each having the default value of 2.0 (though any values between 0.0 and 4.0 can be used), while the value of each is independent of the value of the other. Also, the velocity of a particle for any given dimension is limited to V_{max} (another parameter set by the user) to avoid the particles swarming out of control (something that would destabilize the whole process). The exact value of this parameter depends on the problem.

Other parameters include the number of particles (usually at least 20, with more complex problems usually requiring more particles), the range of the values of the particles (which is dependent on the problem), and the stopping conditions—namely the total number of iterations and the minimum error threshold. These stopping conditions are also dependent on the problem.

To make PSO faster, we can include an additional parameter that affects the progress the algorithm makes as it searches through the solution space. If a certain number of iterations take place without any significant progress in the *objective function*, then the algorithm can terminate; in these cases, the swarm usually has gotten stuck in a local optimum.

Main PSO variants

Just like most well-established algorithms in AI, PSO has its share of variants, most of which are better-suited for certain sets of problems. The most important of these variants are:

- **PSO with inertia** (by Shi and Eberhart): a variation of PSO that uses an "inertia weight" (usually around 0.9), which gradually decreases, allowing for a narrowing of the search over time. This enables PSO to switch from exploratory to exploitative mode, yielding more accurate solutions.

- **PSO with Neighborhood Operator** (by Suganthan): a popular variant of PSO that considers other particles in the same neighborhood. The idea is that through this method the chances of getting trapped in a local optimum are greatly reduced, making the whole system more robust.

- **Discrete PSO** (by Kennedy and Eberhart): a variant of PSO that enables the solution of discrete optimization problems.

- **Constriction PSO** (by Clerc and Kennedy): a version of PSO that doesn't make use of the V_{max} parameter. It manages keep velocities in check by introducing a couple of additional parameters, one of which is the constriction coefficient χ (suggested value: 0.7289). These parameters ensure that the velocity of the algorithm remains manageable, making PSO converge smoothly.

- **Fully informed PSO** (by Mendes et al.): a case of Constriction PSO, where the two parameters are the same; this is generalized to any number of particles. This enables each particle to be influenced by each other particle, making the whole process more stable.

- **Bare-bones PSO** (by Kennedy): a lighter version of the original PSO algorithm, with the whole velocity aspect dropped altogether.

- **Firefly** (by Xin-She Yang): a somewhat different approach to the whole "movement" part of the algorithm. We'll examine this in more detail in the following section.

Note that since PSO is a topic of active research, there are continually new variants being developed. The variants mentioned here are just the few that have stood the test of time; they go on to show that there is a lot of promise in this optimization framework.

Firefly optimizer

The Firefly optimizer is one of the most interesting variants of PSO—in fact, it is unique enough to be considered a different optimizer by many people.

However, when examined in depth, it becomes clear that the Firefly optimizer is a more creative take on the key components of PSO.

Despite sharing the same principles as PSO, a couple of distinct differences give Firefly its niche. For starters, each particle is attracted by all other particles—not just the best-performing one. This is reminiscent of the Fully-Informed PSO variant.

In addition, there is no velocity in this algorithm, since the concept of inertia is replaced by "fogginess." In other words, light is not dispersed perfectly as if in a vacuum (such a case would make the algorithm very unstable and the particles' movement chaotic). This is expressed by the light-absorption coefficient γ, which ensures that the attraction fades exponentially, while the intensity of the light follows the Newtonian model of gravity. The exponential diminishing of the attractiveness of other particles ensures that the fireflies don't get too confused and that it is generally the closest well-performing firefly that has the most impact.

Other than all that, the Firefly algorithm follows the same strategy as the PSO algorithm. You can read about the details of the Firefly algorithm in its documentation.[12]

The key advantages of Firefly over PSO are that it is faster and more accurate, across a variety of objective functions. On the downside, it has a bunch of parameters that need to be set, and tweaking the algorithm is quite a challenge. Fortunately, the Firefly algorithm is good enough to be useful off the shelf with the default parameter values. The code that accompanies this book includes an implementation of Firefly that we'll examine in Chapter 10, when we discuss optimization ensembles.

---

[12] https://arxiv.org/pdf/1308.3898.pdf.

PSO versus other optimization methods

A few optimization methods are similar to PSO, but are not part of its taxonomy. The two most well-known of these are Ant Colony Optimization (ACO) and Genetic Algorithms (GAs). Note that both these algorithms are also part of the Evolutionary Computing (EC) family.

Despite its similarities to PSO, ACO takes a probabilistic approach to optimization. The whole framework resembles a chaotic system, with pheromones playing the role of attractors. Pheromones are the influential forces a solution exercises over other solutions. The potential solutions are called "ants" instead of particles, but the idea is the same. What's more, ACO has spawned its own set of variants and similar methods, such as Bee Colony Optimization (BCO).

As for GAs, they involve a lot of tweaking of solutions, both through random changes and through interactions with other solutions. Furthermore, they involve coding each solution in a binary pattern. We'll explore GA optimization in detail in the next chapter. Although GAs are versatile in terms of the kind of problems they can solve, they are rarely used for optimizing continuous variables. This is because they fail to perform as well as PSOs and other similar methods in the EC family.

PSO implementation in Julia

PSO can be easily implemented in any programming language. For simplicity and performance, we'll be using Julia (ver. 1.0) for this and all the other optimization methods in this book. Note that a PSO implementation is already available on Github.[13] However, it is unlikely that you'll find an implementation more comprehensive than the one we provide here, since few Julia programmers have delved into this topic extensively.

The PSO implementation in this section takes the fitness function as input argument *ff*, which in turn takes as input an array of numbers. This way, there is no way for PSO to know how many variables it deals with, since there is nothing in the function ff to denote that. As a result, the number of variables to optimize needs to be included as well, in its inputs (variable *nv*). It has been found empirically that a swarm size of about 10 times the number of variables works well; this is what *ps,* the number of particles parameter, defaults to. Beyond these, there are a few additional inputs based on what we've discussed previously.

```julia
function pso(ff::Function, nv::Int64, minimize::Bool = true,
    ps::Int64 = 10*nv, ni::Int64 = 2000, c = [2.0, 2.0], maxv =
    2.0, iwp = 50)
    buffer = div(iwp, 2)
    ni += iwp
    tol = 1e-6
    PP = randn(ps, nv)              # population positions
    PV = randn(ps, nv)              # population velocities
    PC = Array{Float64}(undef, ps)  # population costs (scores)
    Pp_best = copy(PP)              # particle's best position
    gb = Array{Float64}(undef, ni)  # global best over time

    if minimize
        temp = Inf
    else
        temp = -Inf
    end

    for I = 1:iwp; gb[i] = temp; end
    for I = 1:ps; PC[i] = ff(PP[I,:][:]); end
    p_best = copy(PC)
```

___

[13] https://bit.ly/2NyIiBv.

```
if minimize
    m, ind = findmin(PC)
else
    m, ind = findmax(PC)
end

gb[1+buffer] = m
Pg_best = PP[ind,:]

for iter = (iwp + 1):ni
    for I = 1:ps
        PV[I,:] += c[1] * rand() * (Pp_best[I,:] - PP[I,:]) +
 c[2] * rand() * (Pg_best - PP[I,:])

        for j = 1:nv
            if PV[I,j] > maxv; PV[I,j] = maxv; end
            if PV[I,j] < -maxv; PV[I,j] = -maxv; end
        end

        PP[I,:] += PV[I,:]
        PC[i] = ff(PP[I,:][:])
        gb[iter] = gb[iter - 1]

        if minimize
            if PC[i] < p_best[i]
                p_best[i] = PC[i]
                Pp_best[I,:] = PP[I,:]

                if PC[i] < gb[iter]
                    gb[iter] = PC[i]
                    Pg_best = PP[I,:]
                end
            end
        else # maximizing mode
            if PC[i] > p_best[i]
                p_best[i] = PC[i]
                Pp_best[I,:] = PP[I,:]

                if PC[i] > gb[iter]
                    gb[iter] = PC[i]
                    Pg_best = PP[I,:]
                end
```

```
            end # of 2ⁿᵈ if
          end # of 1ˢᵗ if
      end # of I loop

      if abs(gb[iter] - gb[iter-iwp]) < tol
          return Pg_best, gb[iter] # best solution and best
    value respectively
      end
    end # of iter loop

    return Pg_best, gb[end] # best solution and best value
    respectively
  end
```

Despite its length, the core of the algorithm is simple, quite fast, and relatively light on computational resources. Note that most of the parameters are optional, since their default values are predefined. Simply feed it the fitness function and the number of variables, and decide whether you want it to be minimized or not. If you don't specify the latter, the PSO method defaults to minimization of the fitness function.

Note that we use here the "vanilla" version of PSO, with minimal add-ons. As a result, its performance is not great. We'll investigate a more improved Julia script of PSO in Chapter 10, along with its parallelized version.

PSO in action

The first practical application of PSO proposed by its creators was training ANNs. However, PSOs flexible nature has made it useful in various other domains, such as combinatorial optimization, signal processing, telecommunications, control systems, data mining, design, power systems, and more. Also, as more specialized algorithms for training ANNs became available, PSO ceased being a relevant option for optimizing the weights of an ANN.

Although most versions of PSO involve a single-objective approach (having a single fitness function), with some changes, PSO can be used in multiple-objective and dynamic problems (with varying configurations). The possibility of having constraints in the solution space has also been explored (the constraints in this latter case are inherently different from the constriction PSO variant).

So, even though PSO was originally a data science-oriented algorithm, its applicability has made it a useful tool for all sorts of problems. This clearly shows how AI is an independent field that dovetails well with almost any data-related scenario.

Nevertheless, some organizational problems require the use of an optimizer, rather than a machine learning system. Examples of such issues include creating an optimal schedule, finding the best way to stock a warehouse, or working out the most efficient route for a delivery driver. These problems are so common in so many industries that familiarity with a robust optimizer like PSO can be a good distinguishing factor, professionally. Besides, having a variety of skills can help you develop a more holistic view of a challenging situation, empowering you to find a better strategy for tackling it.

Note that just like any other AI optimizer, PSO does not provide the best solution to a problem, nor does it have mathematical precision. However, it is very efficient. As such, PSO adds a lot of value in cases where an approximate solution is sufficient, especially if the time it takes to find this solution is also important. Furthermore, when the problems involve functions that cannot be easily analyzed mathematically (e.g. functions that aren't "smooth" enough to calculate a derivative function), a method like PSO is the most viable option.

Minimizing a polynomial expression

The examples of the PSO involve different problems, as expressed by a couple of different fitness functions. In the first case we consider a minimization problem, while in the latter, we'll look at a maximization problem. First, let's start with defining the fitness function, F, for the first problem, which involves a complex (highly non-linear) polynomial expression:

```
function F(X::Array{Float64})
    return y = X[1]^2 + X[2]^2 + abs(X[3]) +
    sqrt(abs(X[4]*X[5])) + 1.0
end
```

You can also write the above function as:

```
F(X::Array{Float64}) = X[1]^2 + X[2]^2 + abs(X[3]) +
    sqrt(abs(X[4]*X[5])) + 1.0
```

Though more compact, this may not be as useful for complex functions involving a lot of variables.

Whatever the case, we expect to get a solution that's close to (0, 0, 0, 0, 0), since this is the solution that corresponds to the absolute minimum of this function (which is in this case 1.0 since $0^2 + 0^2 + |0| + sqrt(|0*0|) + 1 = 1$).

Next, we need to run the PSO algorithm, using the above function as an input. We'll work with the default values for the input parameters, for the majority of them:

```
pso(F, 5)
```

For one of the runs of PSO, the solution [-0.0403686, 0.0717666, -0.0102388, 0.0966982, -0.129386] was yielded, corresponding to a fitness score of approximately 1.243. Although this solution is not particularly impressive, it is decent, considering the complexity of the problem and the fact that we used the most basic version of the optimizer.

We can try a smaller swarm – say, of 20 particles – for comparison:

```
pso(F, 5, true, 20)
```

The result in this case was [0.164684, -0.241848, 0.0640438, -0.0186612, -0.882855], having a fitness score of about 1.388. Additional runs may yield better scores. This shows that PSO systems can yield acceptable results, even without lots of particles.

We can measure how long this whole process takes using the @time meta-command, as follows:

```
@time pso(F, 5)
```

In this case, for a solution of comparable fitness, we learn that the whole process took about 0.008 seconds—not bad at all. As a bonus, we get some information about how many computational resources the process consumes. That is, 7.179 MB of RAM through its 87.6K allocations. Note that for this report to be accurate, the command must run more than once. This is true of all Julia functions benchmarked using this meta-command.

Maximizing an exponential expression

Let's try something a bit more challenging for the maximization example. This problem consists of six variables, one of which is raised to the 4th power, making the solution space a bit rougher.

```
Function F2(X::Array{Float64})
    return y = exp(-X[1]^2) + exp(-X[2]^2) + exp(-abs(X[3])) +
    exp(-    sqrt(abs(X[4]*X[5]))) + exp(-X[6]^4)
end
```

Like in the previous case, we expect to get something close to (0, 0, 0, 0, 0, 0) as a solution, since this is the absolute maximum of this function (which is equal to

5.0 since F2(0, 0, 0, 0, 0, 0) = exp(-0^2) + exp(-0^2) + exp(-|0|) + exp(-sqrt(|0*0}})) + exp(-0^4) = 1 + 1 + 1 + 1 + 1 = 5).

To use PSO, we simply type:

```
pso(F2, 6, false)
```

The solution obtained is [0.370003, 0.0544304, 0.0980422, 0.00426721, -0.011095, 0.294815], corresponding to a fitness score of about 4.721, which is quite close to the maximum value we were expecting.

Again, we can see how much time and computational resources this whole process took in this case:

```
@time pso(F2, 6, false)
```

The time the whole problem took was about 0.009 seconds, while it took about 15.006 MB of memory, and around 183.1K allocations. Clearly, this is a somewhat tougher problem, involving a larger swarm, so it takes a bit more time and memory (though the time overhead is quite small). If we were to solve either one of these problems with a deterministic optimizer, though, it would probably take the same computer longer.

PSO tips

Despite its simplicity, avoiding suboptimal results with PSO requires some attention to detail. For instance, if you use a low value for V_{max}, the algorithm will take a long time to converge (not to mention the increased risk of it getting stuck at a local optimum, yielding a mediocre solution). On the other hand, a very large value would make the whole process very unstable (and unable to converge on any optimum).

Furthermore, a very large number of particles make the whole system fairly slow; too few particles make it difficult to find the optimum solution. The empirical default value of 10 times the number of variables seems to work well for all the benchmarks tried, but it's just a rule of thumb; make sure you experiment with this parameter when you fine-tune your PSO model.

In addition, in some cases, PSO is used with a variable V_{max} parameter, to ensure that it converges more smoothly. For example, you can reduce it by a factor k, every so many iterations, so that as it approaches the optimum value of the function, the particles of the swarm will be closer together, yielding a better precision. Once you get the hang of PSO, you can experiment with such parameters to improve its performance.

What's more, it's a good idea to make sure that the swarm covers a meaningful area when deployed, to ensure that it won't get stuck in a local optimum. In other words, if you are optimizing a set of three parameters that all take place between 0 and 1, it's best to spread the swarm to cover as much volume as possible, instead of having them all close to (0, 0, 0). This is because if the optimal solution is close to (0, 1, 1), for example, it could take the swarm a long time to approach it.

How much area exactly a swarm covers when deployed is something you may want to experiment with, since it largely depends on the problem at hand. Also consider the distribution of the particles across the various dimensions of the problem space. The distribution used in this implementation is Gaussian, as shown through the randn() function used to initialize the particles.

The algorithm's performance can be greatly improved if you parallelize it. The best way to do so involves defining a number of workers, each one undertaking an instance of the algorithm, and then comparing their findings, taking the smaller or larger of their solutions, depending on the type of optimization problem you are solving. Make sure you use the @everywhere meta-command in front of all the functions, however, or the parallelization will not work. We'll further examine the parallelized version of PSO in Chapter 10.

Finally, PSO is still a work in progress, so don't be afraid to experiment a bit, changing it to suit the problem you need to solve. We also recommend you try to implement the Firefly algorithm. We'll be using the latter a bit in Chapter 10, where we'll explore the possibilities of optimization ensembles.

Summary

- Particle Swarm Optimization (PSO) is a fundamental optimization algorithm under the umbrella of nature-inspired optimizers. It is also part of the Computational Intelligence group of systems, which is a subclass of AI.

- PSO entails a set of potential solutions which constantly evolve as a group, becoming better and better, based on some fitness function the system tries to optimize.

- Just like most robust algorithms of this type, PSO is ideal for tackling complex, highly non-linear problems, usually involving many variables, such as the parameters of a complex system like an ANN.

- PSO is noticeably different from Ant Colony Optimization (ACO) as well as from Genetic Algorithms (Gas). There also exist some differences among the variants of PSO; differences mainly concern the scope and the specifics of the method.

- There are various versions of PSO. Firefly is one of the most noteworthy variations, partly due to its distinct approach to the problem space.

- The "swarm" used in Firefly is a set of fireflies, attracted to each other based on how well they perform in the fitness function the swarm is trying to optimize. Instead of using velocities, however, the particles in this case are "pulled" by all of the other particles, based on how far they are and how "bright" they shine.

- Firefly is generally faster and more accurate as an optimizer, compared to PSO (as well as a few other nature-inspired optimizers).

- The original PSO and most of its variants are ideal for optimizing continuous variables.

- The fitness function of an optimizer like PSO does not need to be differentiable, since no derivatives of it are ever calculated.

- PSO has a variety of applications, including ANN training, signal processing, and combinatorial optimization problems. Different versions of PSO can handle more sophisticated optimization scenarios, such as multiple-objective problems, constrains-based cases, and dynamic problems. One version of PSO (Discrete PSO) even tackles discrete optimization problems.

- PSO on its own is not as robust as its variants, but it's very useful to know. Understanding its original form makes learning its variants (or creating new ones) significantly easier.

## CHAPTER 7

Building an Optimizer Based on Genetic Algorithms

The Genetic Algorithm (GA) is a popular optimization method predating most similar approaches to nature-inspired optimizers. It is part of the Evolutionary Computing family of methods, which is a very robust kind of AI. Although this optimization approach was first introduced in the 1960s by Ingo Rechenberg, the GA framework wasn't fully realized until a bit later, in the early 1970s, by John Holland's team. John Holland popularized this new approach with his book *Adaption in Natural and Artificial Systems*, which was published in 1975.

GAs are heavily influenced by Darwinian evolution. The idea behind them is that each solution is part of a group of cells that are evolving over a number of generations (the equivalent of epochs in ANNs and iterations in PSO). As the group evolves, it gets closer and closer to the optimal solution to the optimization problem it models.

We'll examine the specifics of the GA optimization framework and its core algorithm, see how to implement it in Julia, point out several variants, and discuss how Gas are applicable to data science

The idea of the GA framework is to view the problem as a set of discrete elements, forming what is referred to as a *chromosome*. Each one of these elements is referred to as a *gene*, and they can be arbitrary in number, depending on the problem at hand. Although each gene is usually a bit, encoding can take a variety of forms.[14] A collection of all these chromosomes is called a *genome.* Through a series of processes, the genome evolves into the ideal combination of genes. This "perfect combination" is called a "genotype," and it encapsulates the solution we are after. The information captured in each gene encoding is referred to as a *trait.*

Unlike PSO, solution elements of GAs don't change through motion, but through a pair of processes called *mutation* and *crossover.* These terms are again borrowed from biology, as the processes are similar to those that occur in replicating DNA. In nature, this process leads to the birth of new organisms; that's why we refer to different iterations of this evolutionary process as "generations".

Mutation is the simplest process, as it involves a single chromosome. Basically, it ensures that over each *generation,* there is a chance that some gene in the chromosome will change randomly. The probability of this happening is fairly small, but the whole evolutionary process takes so long that it is almost guaranteed to happen at least once. Furthermore, it is theoretically possible to have multiple mutations in the same chromosome (especially if it is large enough). The purpose of the mutation is that it ensures diversity in the traits, which would otherwise remain stagnant.

Crossover (or recombination) is the most common process by which elements change. It involves two chromosomes merging into a single one, at either a random or a predefined location such as the middle, as can be seen in Figure 6.

However, certain instances of crossover can involve two locations, or even a logical operator like AND. For the purposes of simplicity, we'll work with the basic single-point crossover in this chapter.

---

[14] https://bit.ly/2qw8gvZ.

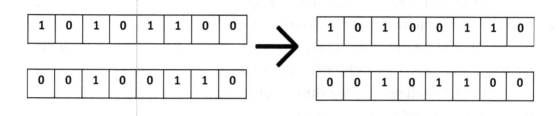

Figure 6. Crossover process for a pair of simple chromosomes. Note that the crossover location can be any point in the chromosome, as well as in multiple points.

The crossover process ensures that the genome changes over time, through traits that already manifest in the parents (e.g. eye color). Which of these traits survive in the long run depends on another aspect of the evolutionary process called *fitness*. Not all chromosomes get to cross over, since there exists a *selection* process to ensure that the best-performing chromosomes are most likely to have descendants in the next generation, much like in a species, only the better equipped individuals (e.g. faster, more adaptable, with better immune systems, etc.) manage to survive and procreate, ensuring that their genes don't die out.

Fitness is the measure of how well these chromosomes perform as potential solutions to the problem we are solving. Just like with PSO, we are trying to maximize or minimize a fitness function that evaluates a solution. As the number of chromosomes must remain constant through the whole evolutionary process (otherwise we'd risk a *population* explosion, draining our computational resources), only the best chromosomes make it to the next generation, based on their fitness.

Elitism is an auxiliary aspect of the GAs framework that is often used to ensure that the best solution is constantly present. It's like a fail-safe, guarding against the possibility that the new genome is worse than that of the previous generation, due to some bad crossovers and/or bad mutations. Elitism makes sure that the best performing chromosome or chromosomes remain in the next generation regardless.

Although elitism was not part of the original GA framework, it is strongly recommended you make use of it, as it has been shown to generally improve the performance of the optimizer. However, if you overdo it with elitism by getting too many well-performing chromosomes to the next generation at the expense of other, not as well-performing chromosomes, you may end up with an overly homogeneous population. This would result in an optimization process that converges prematurely with the yielded solution more likely to be sub-optimal. Note that the elitism option is controlled by a parameter that indicates how many best-performing chromosomes to keep (see *elitism()* function later on).

The search space of problems tackled with GAs ideally involves a huge number of potential solutions to the problem—usually larger than what could be solved analytically. A modest example: if a GA tried to solve a problem where each chromosome has 60 genes represented as bits, it would have 2^{60} or over a billion *billion* potential solutions.

In general, problems that lend themselves to GAs fall under the umbrella of "NP-hard" problems. These are problems whose solving cannot be reduced to a fast process, as they take exponential time. This means that if the dimensionality of the problem increases by a factor of 2, the complexity of the problem is bound to quadruple, or worse.

A typical NP-hard problem with many applications in logistics is the *Traveling Salesman Problem (TSP)*. This involves finding the optimal way to traverse a graph so that at the end of your trip you are back where you started. Despite its simple description, this is an exceptionally difficult problem as the number of nodes in that graph gets larger.

As the scope of these problems makes finding the best solution quite unrealistic, we opt for a "good enough" solution—one that yields a quite large (or small) value for the fitness function we are trying to maximize or minimize.

Standard Genetic Algorithm

Let's now look at the actual algorithm that lies at the core of the GAs framework, the original Genetic Algorithm itself. The main process is as follows:

1. **Initialization stage:** Generate a random population of n chromosomes (potential solutions for the problem). Define Fitness function F() and optimization mode (maximization or minimization). Define stopping conditions such as the maximum number of generations, or minimum progress of fitness over a given number of generations. Define crossover and mutation probabilities (p_c and p_m respectively), as well as selection scheme.

2. **Fitness evaluation:** Evaluate the fitness of each chromosome x in the population by calculating F(x).

3. **New population:** Create a new genome by repeating the following steps until the new set of chromosomes is complete:
    a) **Selection:** Select two parent chromosomes from a population according to their fitness. Namely, select them with a probability p that is proportional to their fitness scores.
    b) **Crossover:** With a crossover probability p_c, cross over the parents to form new offspring (children). If no crossover is performed, the offspring are exact copies of their parents.
    c) **Mutation:** With a mutation probability p_m, mutate new offspring at each position in it.
    d) **Population update:** Place new offsprings in a new population and discard the previous population.

4. **Loop Process:** Repeat steps 2-3 until a stopping condition has been met.

5. **Output results:** Output the best-performing chromosome and its fitness score.

The selection process involves one of two main methods to stochastically determine which chromosomes get to be parents (candidates of the crossover process) and which don't. These are *roulette wheel selection* and *rank selection*.

The first approach involves creating a "wheel" based on the fitnesses of all the chromosomes, by basically normalizing them so that they add up to 1. This normalization takes place based on a scaling function like exp(x) or sqrt(x), depending on the problem at hand. After, we obtain a random number in the [0, 1) interval, and we pick the chromosome corresponding to the wheel section that includes that random number. We then repeat that process one more time to find the other parent.

The rank selection approach uses the *ranking* of the fitness scores instead of the scores themselves. So, the worst performing chromosome will have a value of 1, the second worse a value of 2, and the best one a value of n, where n is the total number of chromosomes. In all the other aspects, it's the same as the roulette wheel approach. The rank selection approach ensures that all chromosomes have a decent chance of getting selected, especially in cases where a small number of chromosomes dominate the population in terms of performance (because they are significantly better than the rest).

With so many parameters in the GA framework, it can be overwhelming to figure out how to use it for your optimization problems. What follows are some rules of thumb for selecting values for these parameters. Naturally, fiddling with these parameters is a great way to learn, but these guidelines will help you at least get started.

As far as crossover is concerned, you can use a probability between 0.8 and 0.95. This means that around 90% of the time, there will be a crossover taking place for a given chromosome.

Regarding mutation probability, a value around 0.005 to 0.01 generally works. Over time, mutation on its own can produce a decent solution without any crossover at all. Setting this too high will result in a highly unstable genome that will change uncontrollably and never converge.

Population size is a bit trickier to set, since a larger population would still work, but take longer for the algorithm to run. That's why having a number of chromosomes equal to the number of genes in a chromosome is generally a good place to start.

When it comes to selection type, generally the roulette wheel method is fine. However, if you find that a small set of chromosomes monopolize the solution process (resulting in largely sub-optimal results for the whole system), then rank selection may be a better option.

Implementation of GAs in Julia

Let's now look at how this algorithm can be implemented in Julia. Below is a sample implementation of a GA, with the elitism add-on included. We've also included a sample fitness function so that you can test it. Note that some variables in this code are abbreviated. These are as follows:

- X = population data (matrix)
- c = coefficients vector for sample function, for testing purposes
- ff = fitness function to maximize
- nv = number of variables to consider
- maximize = whether the function needs to be maximized or not
- ips = initial population size
- s = desired sum of chromosomes in generated population (an optional but useful parameter for certain problems)

- px = probability of event x happening
- ng = number of generations

The code is written to be easily customized whenever needed, as per the functional programming paradigm that Julia follows.

```
function sample_ff(x::Array{<:Real, 1}, c::Array{<:Real, 1} =
    ones(Int64, length(x))) # function to maximize
    z = abs.(x) .* c
    return 1 / (1 + sum(z))
end

ShouldActivate(p::Float64) = rand() < p # activation trigger for
    an event of probability p

evaluation(ff::Function, x::Array{<:Real, 1}) = ff(x)

function scaling(y::Array{Float64, 1}) # scaling fitness function
    values
    y_ = exp(y)
    # y_ = sqrt(y) # another alternative for scaling
    return y_ / sum(y_)
end

function selection(X::Array{<:Real, 2}, y::Array{Float64, 1},
    nv::Int64, ips::Int64)
    y_ = scaling(y)
    c = 0
    ind = 1
    xs = Array{eltype(X)}(undef, 2, nv)
    ys = Array{Float64}(undef, 2)

    while true
        if ShouldActivate(y_[ind])
            c += 1
            xs[c, :] = X[ind, :]
            ys[c] = y[ind]

            if c == 2; return xs, ys; end
        end
```

```julia
        ind += 1
        if ind > ips; ind = 1; end
    end
end

function mutation(x::Array{<:Real, 1}, p::Float64, nv::Int64) #
    change population a bit
    new = false

    for i = 1:nv
        if ShouldActivate(p)
            new = true
            if eltype(x) <: Bool
                x[i] = !x[i]
            else
                x[i] = 1 - x[i]
            end
        end
    end

    return x, new
end

function crossover(xs::Array{<:Real, 2}, ys::Array{Float64, 1},
    p::Float64, nv::Int64)
    d = rand(1:2) # dominant gene
    z = xs[d, :]
    w = ys[d]
    new = false

    if ShouldActivate(p)
        new = true
        r = 3 - d # recessive gene
        q = rand(1:(nv-1))
        z[1:q] = xs[r, 1:q]
        w = [NaN]
    end

    return z, w, new
end
```

```
function elitism(X::Array{<:Integer, 2}, y::Array{Float64, 1},
    n::Int64)
    YX = hcat(y, X)
    YX_sorted = swi(YX)[1]
    X_elite = round.(Int64, YX_sorted[1:n, 2:end])
    y_elite = YX_sorted[1:n, 1]
    return X_elite, y_elite
end

function GeneratePopulation(ips::Int64, nv::Int64, s::Int64 = -1)
    # function for creating original population
    if s == -1
        X = rand(Bool, ips, nv)

        for i = 1:ips
            if sum(X[i,:]) == 0
                X[i,rand(1:nv)] = true
            end
        end
    else
        x = falses(nv)
        for i = 1:s; x[i] = true; end
        X = Array{Bool}(undef, ips, nv)

        for i = 1:ips
            X[i,:] = x[randperm(nv)]
        end
    end

    return X
end

function runga(ff::Function, nv::Int64, ips::Int64 = nv, s::Int64
    = div(nv, 2),
    ng::Int64 = 1000, pm::Float64 = 0.01, pc::Float64 = 0.9,
    pr::Float64 = 0.1) # wrapper function
    X = GeneratePopulation(ips, nv, s)
    y = Array{Float64}(undef, ips)

    for i = 1:ips
        y[i] = evaluation(ff, X[i,:]) # fitness scores of
    population
```

```
    end

    n = round(Int64, ips*pr) # elite size
    X_ = Array{Bool}(undef, ips, nv) # offspring population
    y_ = Array{Float64}(undef, ips) # fitness scores of offspring
     population

    for i = 1:ng
        X_[1:n, :], y_[1:n] = elitism(X, y, n)

        for j = (n+1):ips
            xs, ys = selection(X, y, nv, ips)
            z, w, new1 = crossover(xs, ys, pc, nv)
            z, new2 = mutation(z, pm, nv)

            if new1 || new2
                y_new = evaluation(ff, z)
            else
                y_new = w
            end

            X_[j,:] = copy(z)
            y_[j] = y_new[1]
        end

        X = copy(X_)
        y = copy(y_)
    end

    ind = findmax(y)[2]
    return X[ind, :], y[ind]
end
```

GAs in action

Let's now examine a couple of GAs at work. Before typing any code, make sure you have loaded the packages Random and Statistics from the Base package, as their functions will be used in these examples. You can do this as follows:

```
using Random, Statistics
```

We'll examine two problems using the GAs optimization framework. The first problem helps you get the hang of the method using an example you may have encountered before. The second example is more related to the data science craft, so we'll use our second synthetic dataset for that.

For starters, let's examine an old puzzle problem involving some geometry. We chose this "matchstick problem" since it is easy to comprehend, while at the same time challenging enough to have non-obvious solutions. The goal is to form two squares, limiting the total number of matchsticks used to a maximum of 8.

In the first example, we're looking at a maximization problem. So, given a set of 8 matches, what's the best arrangement so that we have two squares, in a 2x2 grid (Figure 7)?

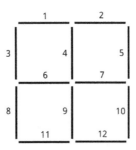

Figure 7. Encoding schema for a 2x2 grid for a match problem. The 12 lines in this diagram represent all possible positions of a match.

We must first define the right fitness function. This may seem a bit of a daunting task, so let's break it down into smaller sub-tasks, each with its own function. (That's one of the strengths of a functional programming language, anyway.) This process may seem a bit overwhelming at first, but at the very least, it's good practice for your analytical skills (which are quite transferable to other aspects of AI and data science).

Let's start by pinpointing all the possible squares, in relation to the indexes of matchsticks, based on the grid illustrated above:

```
global S = [[1, 3, 4, 6], [2, 4, 5, 7], [6, 8, 9, 11], [7, 9, 10,
    12], [1, 2, 3, 5, 8, 10, 11, 12]];
```

Then we can create a function that shows whether the sum of true values in a chromosome is valid or not:

```
IsSumRight(x::Array{Bool, 1}, n::Int64) = (sum(x) == n)
```

In this case, n would be 8. However, it's good practice to make these functions parametric, so that you can experiment with variants of the problem afterwards if needed.

Next, we'll need to create a function that calculates how many squares are formed with the matches from a given chromosome. This would look something like this:

```
function NumberOfSquares(x::Array{Bool, 1})
    z = 0

    for s in S
        q = true

        for i in s
            q = q && x[i]
        end
```

```
            if q; z += 1; end
        end

        return z
    end
```

Also, we'll need a function to help us decipher a chromosome, turning its 1s and 0s into indexes we can interpret using the grid:

```
function MatchIndexes(X::Array{Bool, 1})
    q = collect(1:12) .* X
    return q[q .> 0]
end
```

Now it's time for the actual fitness function, which makes use of all the above auxiliary functions in a way that's meaningful to the problem at hand:

```
function ff1(x::Array{Bool, 1})
    z = 2.0 # fitness score

    if IsSumRight(x, 8)
        z += 1
        Q = MatchIndexes(x)
        OK = true

        for q in Q
            ok = false

            for s in S
                if q in s
                    ok_ = true

                    for s_ in s
                        if !(s_ in Q)
                            ok_ = false
                            break
                        end
                    end

                    if ok_; ok = true; end
```

```
            end
        end

        if !ok
            OK = false
        end
    end

    if !OK; z -= 1.5; end # loose ends in the squares
formation
    s = NumberOfSquares(x)

    if s == 2 # have needed number of squares
        z += 1.0
    elseif s == 1 # have just one square
        z += 0.75
    end
end

    return z

end
```

This function may seem a bit complex because it also scans for loose matchsticks, which it penalizes since they are not part of the desirable solution (i.e. their use would make the problem easier).

Naturally, we'll need to maximize this function. We assign the values we assign to the fitness score of the chromosome for the various states, because even a suboptimal solution needs to be rewarded somehow. Otherwise it would be much more difficult for the optimizer to know if it's going towards the right direction since it would only be able to discern between a great solution and a terrible one. With the intermediate rewards, however, for solutions that are OK (towards the right direction) but still not acceptable, the whole solution landscape becomes smoother and easier for the algorithm to navigate. Also, it's important to avoid using extreme values such as Inf or NaN as part of the fitness function, as this would confuse the whole system during the selection process.

Running the GA algorithm for this problem should be straightforward at this point, though for a problem like this, it is best to use more generations than the default (at least 2500):

```
x, f = runga(ff1, 12, 12, 8, 25000)
println(MatchIndexes(x))
println(f)
```

There are two possible solutions to this problem (which are also symmetrical), and the system correctly identifies one of them:

[2, 4, 5, 6, 7, 8, 9, 11]. This corresponds to the configuration shown in Figure 8:

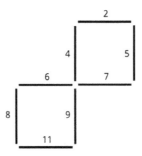

Figure 8. One of the two potential solutions to the matchstick problem described in example 1. The other solution involves a symmetric image of this one.

This solution has a fitness score of 4.0, which is the highest possible. Note that to obtain this solution, you may need to run the optimizer a couple of times at least, since it won't always converge on it. Alternatively, it may converge on a symmetric arrangement, also having a fitness score of 4.0.

For the second example of the GA framework, we'll look at a simple data science problem involving data engineering. Given a set of 40 features, we'll figure out the 20 features that are least correlated to each other. In this case, we'll use the second dataset (consisting of 20 features), along with a set of new features derived from the original 20 ones, using the square root operator. As you might expect, these 20 new features are strongly correlated to the original 20 ones, so 20 of the features of the final feature set should be removed through this whole process.

Let's get started by loading the dataset:

```
data = readcsvfile("data2.csv");
```

Note that you could also load the data using the read() function from the CSV library by typing CSV.read("data2.csv"). However, the custom-made function readcsvfile() used here is somewhat faster as it is customized to the problem at hand. We won't show the code for this method for brevity, but you can find it in the corresponding Jupyter notebook.

Next, we'll need to isolate the features of the dataset, and create the new features that the GA system should be able to identify and eliminate:

```
features = data[:, 1:20]
Z = Array{Float64}(undef, 250000, 40)
Z[:, 1:20] = features
for i = 1:20
    Z[:, 20 + i] = sqrt.(features[:, i])
end
```

Clearly, the new features are going to be correlated to the original ones, which we can verify as follows:

```
cor(Z[:,1], Z[:,21])
```

However, we'll need easy access to all correlations among the various features. As such, it makes sense to compute all these correlations beforehand and store them in a variable that all functions can easily access:

```
global CM = cor(Z);

for i = 1:40
```

```
        CM[i,i] = 0.0
    end
```

Note that we set the correlation of each variable with itself to 0, to avoid allowing that value to dominate all the others.

Now, it's time to define the fitness function for this problem, which should look something like this:

```
function ff2(X::Array{Bool, 1})
    N = length(X)
    f = collect(1:N) .* X
    f = f[f .> 0]
    n = length(f)

    if n != 20
        return -Inf
    end

    y = Array{Float64}(undef, n)

    for i = 1:n
        y[i] = (maximum(abs.(CM[f, f])))
    end

    return -maximum(y)
end
```

In order to find the optimal selection of features, we must ensure that only one version of each feature exists in the final feature set (e.g. by getting rid of all the newer features, or all the older ones, or some combination of both, so that for each one of the original features only one version of it remains in the reduced feature set). As such, we'll need to make the final result of the fitness function negative; this makes the whole process a minimization problem. Upon doing this, we can now run the GAs optimizer as follows:

```
x, f = runga(ff2, 40)
```

To better understand the results, we can do some wrangling:

```
ind = collect(1:40) .* x
println(ind[ind .> 0])
println(f)
```

The outputs in this case are [1, 2, 3, 4, 5, 6, 7, 8, 11, 12, 13, 14, 15, 16, 17, 18, 19, 20, 29, 30] and -0.00505, corresponding to the indexes of the selected features and the corresponding (negative of the) maximum absolute correlation among them. Although this is not the result we expected, it makes sense; in two cases, the original features were substituted with the synthetic ones. Nevertheless, the overall result is perfectly acceptable, since no duplicate features are in the optimized result. Note that due to the inherent randomness of the GAs algorithm, you are bound to obtain slightly different results. However, they should yield a fitness score that's similar to the one obtained here.

Hopefully these examples have demonstrated that you must take special care when encoding a GA model. Contrary to other AI systems of this class, GAs aren't always straightforward when it comes to creating a fitness function and encoding the problem parameters accordingly. Many GAs require additional functions to be coded, to be practical.

Beyond these examples, there are various applications of GAs that make learning them a worthwhile effort. Many of these cases are often referred to as the knapsack problem, which involves finding the optimum collection of items to put in a knapsack, given some weight restrictions and some value for each item. The idea is to maximize the overall value of the collection, while also keeping the total weight under a given threshold, for each container (knapsack).

However, other kinds of problems, including optimization of continuous variables, can be solved using GAs.

For example, GAs can be used in feature selection, as a dimensionality reduction methodology. The restriction in this case would be that the selected features are below a given proportion of the original feature set, while at the same time capturing as much information of the original feature set as possible. Naturally, in cases with a lot of features, selecting a good subset of those features can be quite challenging due to the enormous amount of combinations that are possible—which is exactly where GAs come in handy.

In addition, GAs can be used in all kinds of situations where discrete optimization is required, such as non-linear dynamic systems. One such case is the stock market, where GAs can be used to select the best stocks for a portfolio. Naturally, building a portfolio this way would require some additional analysis to determine the value of each stock, but GAs can play an important role in the selection process itself, once those values have been established.

GAs can also be used in other optimization scenarios, such as scheduling. Building an optimal schedule around many restrictions and preferences is a classical discrete optimization problem, applicable nearly everywhere from project management to logistics. As long as the problem is properly encoded, GAs can be very effective at finding a solution.

An application closer to data science is the use of GAs to design ANNs, both in terms of architecture and in terms of weights (training). Although PSO can be great at figuring out the weight values, it isn't best suited for working out the architecture of an ANN. As we saw in the first chapters of this book, the architecture of such a network involves the number of neurons in each layer, as well as how they are connected (and not all ANNs have a dense connectivity).

Finally, GAs are used for biological research, as in the case of finding the shape of a protein molecule. This is particularly useful for the research of potential treatments for cancer, since the closely-linked problem of protein folding is an NP-hard problem with a huge solution space.

There are several more applications beyond these, some more specialized than others. The fact that GAs find use in such a broad spectrum of domains is a testament to their versatility and value .

Main variants of GAs

The GA is a very general framework, so the standard algorithm we saw earlier has several variations that perform better in many cases.

One such variant is the Hybrid Genetic Algorithms (HGAs), which is basically an ensemble approach to GAs, executed in sequential fashion (we'll talk about PSO-related optimization ensembles in detail in Chapter 10). The standard GA is combined with a different optimizer that is better suited for finding an optimum in a smaller solution space, usually using derivatives or any other additional information regarding the fitness function. GA is applied globally and once a local optimum is found, the other optimizer takes over to refine the solution. HGAs are useful when the fitness function can be differentiated, or when a more accurate solution is required.

Another interesting variant is the Self-Organizing Genetic Algorithm (SOGA). As their name suggests, SOGAs involve a process whereby the parameters of the optimization method are also optimized, along with the variables of the problem at hand. So, instead of fine-tuning the optimization model yourself, the model does it for you.

The Variable Selective Pressure Model (VSPM) is a newer variant of GAs worth considering. This relatively sophisticated approach to GAs involves changing the selection strategy so that you can steer how much diversity exists in the population, thereby avoiding overly homogeneous or overly diverse populations. The idea is to introduce an "infant mortality" rate that limits the presence of weaker chromosomes in the population.

Genetic programming

Moreover, *Genetic Programming (GP)* is a powerful GA variant that focuses on continuous variables. As it is quite distinct from the standard GA, and since its usefulness in data science applications is noteworthy, we'll take a closer look at GP.

Finally, any add-on to the standard GA, such the elitism process, can be viewed as a variant of sorts. After all, the broad framework lends itself to tweaking, so if you delve into it a bit, you are bound to come up with your own variant of the optimization method.

Genetic Programming is an interesting variant of GAs, which has received a lot of attention in the past few years. It involves "building" a synthetic function off other simpler functions that take the form of genes. However, there is also some data that is used in those functions, so the inputs of a GP model include a couple of data streams, one for the inputs and one for the outputs of the function that needs to be approximated.

Note that this problem can be solved with a regression model, though the model's success will be quite limited by linear combinations. Of course, you can have a non-linear regression model, but you'd have to create the non-linear features yourself (which takes considerable effort). You could also use an ANN, but you wouldn't be able to see how the inputs are mapped to the outputs (just like the "black box" issue we discussed in previous chapters). If you require a mapping through a function that you can view in its entirety, GP is the best way to go.

However, the function that GP yields is not necessarily a good model since it is bound to overfit if you use the error as a fitness function (which you'd minimize afterwards). That's why it would make more sense to use some heuristic, such as the correlation coefficient or a similarity metric in general, as the fitness function (which you'd maximize in this case). Such problems have been solved successfully for feature fusion scenarios, as part of a predictive analytics model.[15]

The functions that GP uses can be anything from a simple polynomial to some complex trigonometrical function. They must be in their most basic form, since more complex functions will inevitably emerge through the evolution process of the GP system. For example, if you have the functions $\tan(x)$, x^2, and x^3, GP will at one point have chromosomes consisting of $\tan(x^2)$, $\tan(x^3)$, $(\tan(x))^2$, x^6, etc. That's why special care must be taken when selecting those functions so that the data used with them makes sense. For instance, no point in using $sqrt(x)$ if you have data points of negative x, though $sqrt(abs(x))$ could be used instead.

GP is a truly ingenious method that often adds more value than the conventional GA variants, opening new possibilities. Apart from feature fusion, it has been used for building LISP programs. Don't let the fact that many AI experts don't know about GP deter you from trying it out.

GA framework tips

Although useful, many GAs are not so straightforward; you must be aware of several considerations. For starters, as GAs have a lot of parameters, some fine-tuning is usually necessary. Sometimes configuring a GA properly is a big part of its effectiveness, especially in complex problems.

[15] Unfortunately, NDA restrictions prohibit the discussion of details about such problems.

Also, even though GAs are capable of handling continuous optimization problems, they are generally not that effective in those situations. That's why if you want to tackle such problems you have to either use some other optimization framework, or some specialized variant of GAs, such as GP.

Moreover, the standard GA is not all that robust, compared to its variants. So, if you are to use the GA framework for a complex problem, it is best to explore the algorithm's various add-ons, so that you get a more effective and more efficient optimization system.

Furthermore, just like PSO, GAs are great if your fitness function cannot be differentiated, or the process of differentiating is very expensive computationally. However, if you have easy access to the derivatives of the fitness function, other optimization methods may be more effective for finding an accurate solution.

Summary

- The Genetic Algorithm (or GA) is an evolutionary computation framework. These algorithms mimic the biology of genetic reproduction in order to model optimization problems. Here, chromosomes represent potential solutions.

- The bulk of all the chromosomes are called the genome and it progresses in terms of fitness over several iterations called generations.

- GAs involve two main processes for evolving the solutions into something closer to the optimum they are after. These are mutation and crossover.

- Mutation is the process according to which at any given generation, a chromosome may change at a random gene, by flipping its value. Mutation ensures that the genome doesn't get stagnant and therefore the solutions are limited to a particular part of the search space.

- Crossover is the process whereby two chromosomes A and B merge to form two other chromosomes, each consisting of a part of A and a part of B. The split of the parent chromosomes can happen either at a random or a predefined position. Crossover ensures that the solutions are dynamic and therefore able to evolve over time.

- The best-performing chromosome (or chromosomes) is sometimes retained in the next generation. This ensures that the best solution doesn't degrade when the crossovers, mutations, or selections don't work out favorably. This process is called elitism.

- The original Genetic Algorithm involves creating a population of chromosomes, evaluating them using a fitness function, stochastically selecting some of them based on their fitness scores, applying crossover and mutation to them based on these selections, creating a new population based on the results, and repeating this process for a given number of generations or until some other stopping criterion has been met.

- Special care must be taken during the encoding part of a GAs model, since it's not always straightforward, while some additional functions may need to be coded.

- Some of the main variants of GAs include Hybrid GAs, Self-organizing GAs, Variable Selective Pressure Models, and Genetic Programming.

- Genetic Programming (GP) is a very useful variant of the GA. In GPs, different functions are used as chromosomes, in order to create a synthetic function that approximates a given mapping (like a regression system). GP has been used for feature fusion, among other applications.

- Although GAs can handle continuous variables (with the proper encoding), they are not as accurate as other AI systems, such as PSO and Simulated Annealing.

- GAs are ideal for cases where the fitness function cannot be differentiated or the differentiation process is too computationally expensive.

CHAPTER **8**

Building an Optimizer Based on Simulated Annealing

The last (but definitely not least) of all the optimization methods covered in this book is one that has been around for quite a while now. Created in the 1983s by Dr. S. Kirkpatrick and his associates,[16] Simulated Annealing (SA) has been an optimizer ahead of its time. Although some trace this optimizer back to the 1950s as a variant of Monte Carlo, it was officially recognized as an independent optimizer in the 1980s. It makes use of concepts that only came about in some variants of PSO and other, more modern optimizers. Also, even though it has been around in some form or another for over half a century, it only became popular in the 1980s, when computational intelligence started to take off.

Just like swarms and genetics, the natural phenomenon of "annealing" inspired the name of this type of optimizer. Annealing is a term in thermodynamics referring to the cooling process of liquids, related to crystal formation. Simulated Annealing applies this concept to mathematical functions.

At the core of the annealing process emulated by SA is temperature: a control parameter for the whole process. Temperature starts with a fairly high value (such as 10,000 degrees), and then it gradually falls, usually at a geometric rate. Through all this, the energy level of the liquid also falls, as it gradually takes a

---

[16] http://bit.ly/2Oac0fP.

solid form. This represents the value of the fitness function, which is generally minimized (although maximization is also possible).

As the temperature is relatively high, larger changes in the search space are possible; this makes the exploration of more potential solutions feasible, at least in the beginning of the process. Once the temperature gets lower, exploration is diminished, as the method favors exploitation of the search space; later, the algorithm prefers to refine the solutions discovered.

Thermodynamic context aside, this strategy is closer to what we do when we, as humans, solve an optimization problem. First, we try to find a "good-enough" solution that may be crude but still somewhat useful, and then we try to make this solution better by playing around with the corresponding parameters.

SA has been viewed as a major improvement of the "hill climbing" optimization method, which opts for the best possible improvement of the fitness function, at any given point. The rudimentary hill climbing approach to optimization may work for simple functions, but when the search space is more challenging, it is one of the worst optimization strategies out there. SA is said to emulate the hill climbing algorithm towards the end of its search, when it tries to "zero in" on the optimum of the function after having identified its neighborhood (where the search space is more manageable).

The main advantage of the SA method is that it is quite robust, in the sense that it avoids local optima (see Figure 9). This is particularly useful in cases where the solution space is not clear-cut, as the fitness function is quite complex. This feature of SA, along with the fact that it is quite simple, makes it a powerful option for the optimization of such problems. Furthermore, the standard SA algorithm (which we'll examine in a moment) can be further improved by other procedures, making it even more effective.

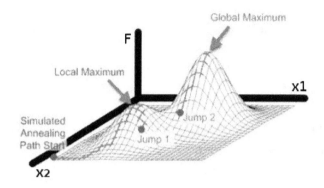

Figure 9. An example of a SA search for a maximization problem involving two variables, x1 and x2. The random solutions picked in the neighborhood of the best solution at a given time, called "jumps", through the search are made possible by the optimizer's willingness to try out new solutions while the temperature is relatively high. This results in SA being able to avoid local optima, like the local maximum in this case, and eventually converge at the global optimum. Plot based on original image created by Max Dama (www.maxdama.com).

The downside of SA is mainly the fine-tuning of the parameters involved. Although most optimization algorithms have a set of default values for these parameters, SA doesn't; there are no "rules of thumb" that generally work. The initial temperature is particularly challenging to define. The rate at which it falls is also a matter of debate, and can vary greatly from problem to problem. So, even though SA can be quite fast in converging, it can have long computation times (if not properly configured) as the search slowly "cools down" to a solution.

For more information on SA, from a more formalized perspective, you can check out the paper "Simulated Annealing" by Professor D. Bertsimas and Professor J. Tsitsiklis, which was published at the Statistical Science journal in 1993.[17]

---

[17] https://bit.ly/2I9fOei.

Pseudo-code of the Standard Simulated Annealing Algorithm

Let's now examine at the steps of the standard SA algorithm. In a nutshell, the process looks like this:

1. Define the optimization mode (minimization or maximization), initial temperature, temperature decrease rate, radius of neighborhood for each variable, and initial solution vector.

2. Propose an updated solution in the same neighborhood and evaluate it using the fitness function.

3. Accept updates that improve this solution.

4. Accept some updates that don't improve this solution. This "acceptance probability" depends on the temperature parameter.

5. Drop the temperature.

6. Repeat steps 2-5 until the temperature has reached zero, or a predefined minimum temperature.

7. Output the best solution found.

During the iterations, it's important to keep in mind the following points:

*   When selecting a new update for the solution, you first need to randomly pick a data point in the search space (representing a potential solution) from the predefined neighborhood area.

*   The new solution may not necessarily be better, as there is a chance that a sub-optimal update may take place, based on the temperature.

- The cooling is typically geometric; it involves a cooling parameter β which usually takes values between 0.8 and 0.99. The higher β is, the slower the cooling. At an iteration k the temperature is $T_k = \beta\ T_{k-1}$. If this cooling strategy is employed, make sure you have a non-zero positive value for the minimum temperature set, to ensure that the search will eventually "cool off."

- The acceptance probability is $p = \exp(-\Delta C\ /\ T)$, where ΔC is the difference in fitness function values between the current and previous solutions, and T is the temperature at that time.

- If cooling is sufficiently slow, the global optimum will be reached eventually. However, this is bound to take some time.

Implementation of Simulated Annealing in Julia

Let's now explore how we can implement a practical version of SA in Julia. We can start with some auxiliary functions:

```julia
function sample_ff(x::Array{<:Real, 1}, c::Array{Int64, 1} =
    ones(Int64, length(x))) # function to maximize
    z = abs.(x) .* c
    return 1 / (1 + sum(z))
end

function SelectNeighbor(x::Array{<:Real, 1}, nv::Int64,
    r::Array{Float64, 1} = ones(nv))
    y = Array{eltype(x)}(undef, nv)

    for i = 1:nv
        y[i] = x[i] + (1 - 2*rand())*r[i]
    end
```

```
        return y
    end

    function ChancePick(absDE::Float64, T::Float64)
        z = exp(absDE / T)
        return rand() < z
    end
```

Note that the sample_ff() function is not essential, but it's useful to have a fitness function to test the algorithm with, to make sure that it works properly. Also, the neighbor function is not entirely necessary as an independent function. However, since that's a weak point of the SA algorithm (and hasn't been explained properly in any of the sources of the algorithm we've found), it would be best to have it as an auxiliary function so that we can explore it more. After all, in an optimization problem, not all variables are of the same scale. It's helpful to have different radius options for each variable's neighborhood, which is possible through the *SelectNeighbor()* function and its r parameter.

With all that out of the way, we can now look at the SA algorithm itself, which can be coded as follows:

```
    function SA(ff::Function, nv::Int64, maximize::Bool = true,
        x::Array{<:Real, 1} = rand(nv), T::Float64 = 1e4,
        beta::Float64 = 0.9, Tmin::Float64 = 1e-9, r::Array{Float64,
        1} = 0.5*ones(nv))
        x = map(Float64, x)
        E = ff(x)
        E_best = E
        x_best = copy(x)

        while T > Tmin
            x_n = SelectNeighbor(x, nv, r)
            E_n = ff(x_n)
            DE = E_n - E

            if (maximize && DE >= 0)||(!maximize && DE <= 0)
                x = copy(x_n)
                E = E_n
```

```
    elseif ChancePick(abs(DE), T)
        x = copy(x)
        E = E_n
    end

    if (maximize && (E > E_best))||(!maximize && (E <
E_best))
        E_best = E
        x_best = x
    end

    T *= beta
end

return x_best, E_best
```

end

Notice that in this implementation of the SA method, we maintain a record of the best solution found. This was not present in the original algorithm, perhaps because at the time that the SA algorithm came about, people weren't fully aware of how stochastic search algorithms behaved, and incorrectly assumed these algorithms always veer towards an improved solution. Other implementations of the SA optimizer maintain a similar strategy of keeping a record of the best solution, since without this add-on the SA algorithm wouldn't perform as well.

If you prefer a more established package for the SA framework, you can also make use of the *Optim.jl* package, which is well-maintained and covers a variety of optimization systems in Julia. It also has decent documentation for the algorithms it covers. For SA in particular, you can use the *SimulatedAnnealing()* function, explained in such documentation.[18]

---

[18] https://bit.ly/2GdhJBW.

Simulated Annealing in action

SA has a variety of applications, usually involving challenging problems. A classical application is graph traversal, as in the case of the Traveling Salesman Problem. This straightforward problem quickly escalates in complexity as the number of nodes in the graph increases, making it difficult to tackle with conventional optimizers. So far, SA and GAs are the best practical methods of solving it.

SA is also used in the realm of Bioinformatics, including the design of protein molecules for 3-D representations. This is an NP kind of problem, sharing the same computational challenges as the Traveling Salesman Problem one, which is why it is usually tackled with advanced optimization methods.

SA's applications also include the design of printer circuit boards, as well as robotics logistics. Both types of problems are particularly challenging and cannot be solved effectively with standard optimizers. Also, for logistics problems, the solution time is of the essence; therefore optimization methods like SA are often preferred.

Beyond these domains, SA has applications in all areas involving problems with complex search spaces, having various local optima. In such scenarios, most common optimizers under-perform or take too long to converge, making algorithms like SA the most practical options available.

Let's now examine how this SA program works in practice, through a couple of examples of minimization and maximization.

In the first example, we'll use a fairly simple function that we'll try to optimize using SA. Namely, a four-variable function ff1, which consists of two cosines and a joint absolute, taking the following form:

```
ff1(x::Array{<:Real, 1}) = (cos(x[1]) + 2)*(cos(x[2]) + 3) +
    abs(x[3]*x[4])
```

This function has a global minimum of 2.0, for the solutions $[\pi, \pi, 0, R]$ and $[\pi, \pi, R, 0]$, where R is any real number. However, due to the nature of the search space, these two groups of solutions are not so obvious—not to an optimization algorithm, anyway.

For this problem we'll start with the potential solution x = [2, 4, 1, -1], which has a value of 4.716. That's pretty bad, but we don't want to make it too easy for the algorithm! We don't *need* to provide SA with a starting position. Doing so, though, gives us a better understanding of how the optimizer performs. Otherwise, if we give it a random solution, it may make things too easy, misleading us about algorithm's performance. Running the SA function on this data is quite straightforward:

```
SA(ff1, 4, false, x)
```

This yields a solution and corresponding fitness function value of [3.13373, 3.10918, 0.0130858, -0.683512], 2.00953, which is not bad at all. The last variable (x_4) is irrelevant in this scenario (since it is covered by variable x_3, in the fitness function), while all the other ones that contribute to the solution are fairly close to the actual minimum the algorithm was after.

The second example tackles an equally challenging function, involving a couple of trigonometric expressions as well as a simple polynomial. This function, which we'll call ff2, takes the following form in Julia:

```
ff2(x::Array{<:Real, 1}) = -x[1]^2 + 2 / (1 + abs(tan(x[2]))) -
    cos(x[3])
```

Naturally, it has a global maximum of 3.0, which corresponds to the solution [0, 0, π]. Since we want to push the algorithm to its limits, we'll start with a potential solution of x = [1, -1, 2], which corresponds to a pretty terrible fitness score of about 0.198. Let's now make use of the SA function, to see how this solution can be improved. For this problem it takes the form:

```
SA(ff2, 3, true, x)
```

A solution it yields is [0.0731461, -0.00582237, 2.93553] which has a fitness score of 2.96192—a big improvement, and quite close to the global maximum.

Main Variants of Simulated Annealing

Unlike other optimization systems, SA doesn't have many variants. The three key flavors are described here:

1. **Deterministic SA.** Although SA is stochastic by design, there is a variant of it that is deterministic. The key benefit of it is that it is faster than the standard SA method. However, it cannot guarantee the optimum solution to the problem it is tackling. Deterministic SA has been applied to clustering problems, particularly the Fuzzy C-means approach to it, an alternative to the well-known K-means algorithm, using Fuzzy Logic.[19]

2. **Adaptive SA.** This variant tackles the issue of having too many parameters to configure, by using heuristics to handle the temperature scheduling. This makes this variant more efficient than the standard SA algorithm and somewhat easier to use. Adaptive SA also has a parallel processing version, which is even more efficient.

3. **Quantum Annealing.** This is a somewhat different approach to the whole problem, though it borrows all the key elements of the standard SA algorithm. The main difference is that Quantum Annealing uses "quantum fluctuations"

---

[19] http://bit.ly/2MiIfZM.

(instead of thermal fluctuations) to bypass irregular areas in the landscape of the search space in relation to the fitness function. Note that the physical process of quantum annealing is what's used in D-Wave's quantum computers and what makes them "quantum" even though other quantum properties could also be used in such a computer.

Simulated Annealing Optimizer tips

Although the SA optimization framework has been tested thoroughly for several years, there are still things to keep in mind. Contrary to most modern optimizers, SA is not created with practicality in mind; as such, a lot of fine-tuning is required for it to work well. If you plan to use this optimization approach, make sure you spend some time configuring it properly, before accepting its proposed solution as truth.

Sometimes when hunting for a good solution, much like a hound going after some game, an SA will stray off the trail and fail to find anything of value. If this happens, you can implement an add-on called a "restart," whereby the system can decide to regress to a significantly better solution, if the solutions it is veering towards are not any better. There are several factors to consider before executing a "restart." It inevitably slows down the search, so make sure you know the algorithm quite well before implementing such a strenuous add-on.

Finally, it is best to start with high temperatures when using SA, as these are guaranteed to provide you with a good solution. If the algorithm takes way too long, you can always speed up the cooling rate or start with a lower temperature. Whatever the case, be aware of this trade-off between effectiveness and speed in the SA algorithm.

Summary

- Simulated Annealing (SA) is a simple, robust, and efficient algorithm for optimization.

- SA emulates the cooling process of liquids as they form crystals to optimize the whole search process. As the temperature is high, SA focuses on exploring more of the solution space; as it "cools down," it focuses on refining the solutions it's already found. This way, it usually avoids becoming trapped in local optima.

- The standard SA algorithm can guarantee an optimum solution if the cooling rate is low enough.

- A few variants of SA include deterministic SA, adaptive SA, and quantum annealing. Each of these methods has unique advantages over the core SA algorithm.

- There are various applications of SA, such as graph traversal, Bioinformatics, designing of printer circuit boards, and logistics for Robotics use cases. SA is especially good to solve "NP" problems, which have various optima, making them especially challenging.

- The "restart" add-on of the SA method, which allows for reverting to a "good" solution in case of having "gone down a wrong trail" in the search, can be useful. However, deciding when to apply a restart is not a trivial task.

- SA is best suited for complex problems having multiple optima, most of which are local optima whose fitness values are substandard for the optimization application we are working with.

## CHAPTER 9

Building an Advanced Deep Learning System

In the previous chapters, we discovered how to build deep learning models using MXNet, TensorFlow, and Keras frameworks. Recall that the models we used in those chapters are known as Artificial Neural Networks, or ANNs for short. Recent research on ANNs has uncovered a broad type of neural networks that have special architectures, different than that of ANNs.

In this chapter, we introduce two of the most popular alternative architectures, which are quite useful for tasks like image classification and natural language translation.

The first model we mention is the *Convolutional Neural Network*. These models perform well in *computer vision*-related tasks; in some domains, like image recognition, it has already surpassed human performance. The second model we cover is the *Recurrent Neural Network*, which is very convenient for sequence modeling, including machine translation and speech recognition. Although we restrict our attention to these two types of neural networks in this chapter, you can read more on other prominent network architectures in the appendices of this book.

Convolutional Neural Networks (CNNs)

One of the most interesting DL systems is the Convolutional Neural Network (usually called CNNs, though some use the term ConvNets). These are DL networks that are very effective in solving image- or sound-related problems, particularly within the classification methodology.

Over the years, though, their architecture has evolved and applicability has expanded to include a variety of cases, such as NLP (natural language processing—the processing and classification of various human sentences). Furthermore, convolutional layers used in CNNs can be integrated as components of more advanced DL systems, such as GANs (see Appendix D). Let's start by describing the architecture and the building blocks of CNNs.

CNN components

CNNs have evolved considerably since their introduction in the 1980s. However, most of them use some variation of the *LeNet architecture*, which was introduced by Yann LeCun and flourished in the 1990s. Back then, CNNs were used primarily for character recognition tasks; this niche changed as they become more versatile in other areas like object detection and segmentation.

Figure 10 shows a simple CNN architecture, geared towards image classification. It is composed of several layers, each specialized in some way. These layers eventually develop a series of meta-features, which are then used to classify the original data into one of the classes that are represented as separate neurons in the output layer. In the output layer, usually a function like sigmoid is used to calculate scores for each class. Those scores can be interpreted as probabilities. For example, if the score for the first class is 0.20 we can say that the probability of the observation belong to the first class is 20%.

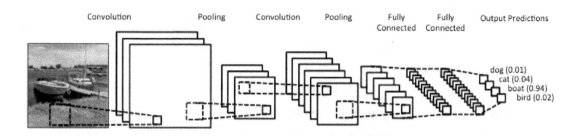

Figure 10. A graphical depiction of an image-focused CNN at work, based on the LeNet architecture. Notice how each neural layer of the network is slightly different, in order to better summarize the data in the image file. The output layer corresponds to the 4 different classes of this classification problem, with the float number in the corresponding neurons corresponding to the probability of the original image being in that particular class. Source of graphic: www.clarifai.com.

Data flow and functionality

The data in a CNN flows the same way as in a basic DL system like an MLP. However, a CNN's functionality is characterized by a series of key operations that are unique for this type of DL network. Namely, functionality is described in terms of:

1. Convolution
2. Non-linearity (usually through the *ReLU* function, though *tanh* and *sigmoid* are also viable options)
3. Pooling (a special kind of sub-sampling)
4. Classification through the fully connected layer(s)

We'll go over each of these operations below. Before that, note that all the data of the original image (or audio clip, etc.) takes the form of a series of integer features. In the case of an image, each one of these features corresponds to a particular pixel in that image. However, CNN can also use sensor data as input, making it a very versatile system.

Convolution

This is where CNNs get their name. The idea of convolution is to extract features from the input image in a methodical and efficient manner. The key benefit of this process is that it considers the spatial relationships of the pixels. This is accomplished by using a small square (aka the *"filter"*) that traverses the image matrix in pixel-long steps. Figure 11 below demonstrates the convolution operator:

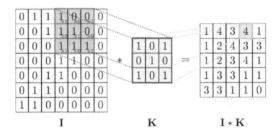

Figure 11. A basic visualization of the convolution operation. I is the input and K is the filter matrices. Source: https://bit.ly/2NToxFh.

From a programmatic point of view, it is helpful to think of the input to a convolutional layer as a two-dimensional matrix (represented as matrix I in Figure 11). In effect, the convolution operation is just a series of matrix multiplications, where the filter matrix is multiplied by a shifted part of the input matrix each time, and the elements of the resulting matrix are summed. This simple mathematical process enables the CNN system to obtain information regarding the local aspects of the data analyzed, giving it a sense of context, which it can leverage in the data science task it undertakes.

The output of this process is represented by a series of neurons comprising the feature map. Normally, more than one filter is used to better capture the subtleties of the original image, resulting in a feature map with a certain "depth" (which is basically a stack of different layers, each corresponding to a filter).

Non-linearity

Non-linearity is essential in all DL systems and since convolution is a linear operation, we need to introduce non-linearity in a different way. One such way is the ReLU function which is applied to each pixel in the image. Note that other non-linear functions can also be used, such as the hyperbolic tangent (tanh) or the sigmoid. Descriptions of these functions are in the glossary.

Pooling

Since the feature maps and the results of the non-linear transformations to the original data are rather large, in the part that follows, we make them smaller through a process called *pooling*. This involves some summarization operation, such as taking the maximum value (called "max pooling"), the average, or even the sum of a particular neighborhood (e.g. a 3x3 window). Various experiments have indicated that max pooling yields the best performance. Finally, the pooling process is an effective way to prevent overfitting.

Classification

This final part of a CNN's functionality is almost identical to that of an MLP which uses softmax as a transfer function in the final layer. As inputs, the CNN uses the meta-features created by pooling. Fully-connected layers in this part of the CNN allow for additional non-linearity and different combinations of these high-level features, yielding a better generalization at a relatively low computational cost.

Training process

When training a CNN, we can use various algorithms; the most popular is backpropagation. Naturally, we must model the outputs using a series of binary vectors, the size of which is the number of classes. Also, the initial weights in all the connections and the filters are all random. Once the CNN is fully trained, it can be used to identify new images that are related to the predefined classes.

Visualization of a CNN model

Visualizing a CNN is often necessary, as this enables us to better understand the results and decide whether the CNN has been trained properly. This is particularly useful when dealing with image data, since we can see how the CNN's perception of the input image evolves through the various layers. Figure 12 shows an example of such a visualization of a CNN.

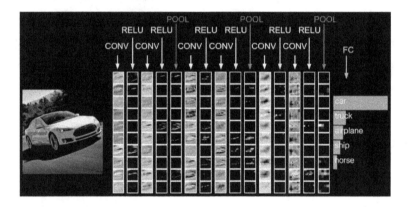

Figure 12. A basic visualization of a CNN used to analyze an image and predict what kind of object it depicts. Source: https://bit.ly/2uBGKOR.

CNNs in action

Now it's time to see just how CNNs work with a real-world problem. Here we provide an image classification example of CNNs using Python and Keras. In the example, we use one of the most popular databases in image recognition, which is the MNIST dataset. This dataset consists of handwritten digits from 0 to 9. Our task is to discern the true digit from the images that include handwritten characters. Figure 13 shows examples from the MNIST dataset.

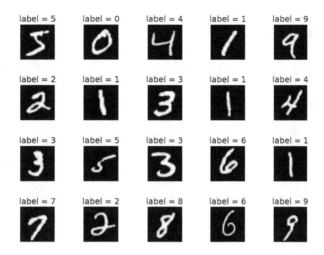

Figure 13. Example images and their associated labels from the MNIST dataset. Source: https://bit.ly/2uoSl4f.

We'll see that Keras' datasets module already provides this dataset, so no additional download is required. The code below is taken from the official Keras repository.[20]

As usual, we begin by importing the relevant libraries. We should also import the MNIST dataset from the datasets module of Keras:

```
from __future__ import print_function
import keras
from keras.datasets import mnist
from keras.models import Sequential
from keras.layers import Dense, Dropout, Flatten
from keras.layers import Conv2D, MaxPooling2D
from keras import backend as K
```

Then we define the batch size as 128, the number of classes as 10 (the number of digits from 0 to 9), the epochs to run the model as 12, and the input image dimension as (28,28), since all of the corresponding images are 28 by 28 pixels:

---

[20] https://bit.ly/2qfAjPM.

```
batch_size = 128
num_classes = 10
epochs = 12
img_rows, img_cols = 28, 28
```

Next, we obtain the MNIST data and load it to variables, after splitting as train and test sets:

```
(x_train, y_train), (x_test, y_test) = mnist.load_data()
```

It is time for some pre-processing—mostly reshaping the variables that hold the data:

```
if K.image_data_format() == 'channels_first':
    x_train = x_train.reshape(x_train.shape[0], 1, img_rows,
     img_cols)
    x_test = x_test.reshape(x_test.shape[0], 1, img_rows,
     img_cols)
    input_shape = (1, img_rows, img_cols)
else:
    x_train = x_train.reshape(x_train.shape[0], img_rows,
     img_cols, 1)
    x_test = x_test.reshape(x_test.shape[0], img_rows, img_cols,
     1)
    input_shape = (img_rows, img_cols, 1)
x_train = x_train.astype('float32')
x_test = x_test.astype('float32')
x_train /= 255
x_test /= 255
print('x_train shape:', x_train.shape)
print(x_train.shape[0], 'train samples')
print(x_test.shape[0], 'test samples')
```

Then we convert the vectors that hold classes into binary class matrices:

```
y_train = keras.utils.to_categorical(y_train, num_classes)
y_test = keras.utils.to_categorical(y_test, num_classes)
```

After these steps, we are now ready to build our graph, using a sequential model. We first add two convolutional layers on top of each other, then we apply the max-pooling operation to the output of the second convolutional layer. Next, we apply dropout. Before we feed the resulting output to the dense layer, we flatten our variables, to comply with the input shapes of the dense layer. The output of this dense layer is regulated with dropout; the resulting output is then fed into the last dense layer for classification. The softmax function is used to turn the results into something that can be interpreted in terms of probabilities. Here is the code snippet of the model building part:

```
model = Sequential()
model.add(Conv2D(32, kernel_size=(3, 3),
                 activation='relu',
                 input_shape=input_shape))
model.add(Conv2D(64, (3, 3), activation='relu'))
model.add(MaxPooling2D(pool_size=(2, 2)))
model.add(Dropout(0.25))
model.add(Flatten())
model.add(Dense(128, activation='relu'))
model.add(Dropout(0.5))
model.add(Dense(num_classes, activation='softmax'))
```

We next compile our model using cross-entry loss and the Adadelta optimization algorithm. We use accuracy as the evaluation metric, as usual:

```
model.compile(loss=keras.losses.categorical_crossentropy,
              optimizer=keras.optimizers.Adadelta(),
              metrics=['accuracy'])
```

It is time to train our model on the training set that we separated from the original MNIST dataset before. We just use the fit() function of the model object to train our model:

```
model.fit(x_train, y_train,
          batch_size=batch_size,
          epochs=epochs,
          verbose=1,
          validation_data=(x_test, y_test))
```

Finally, we evaluate the performance of our model on the test set:

```
score = model.evaluate(x_test, y_test, verbose=0)
print('Test loss:', score[0])
print('Test accuracy:', score[1])
```

After 12 epochs, our model reaches 99% accuracy on the test set—a quite satisfactory result for a simple model like this. This example demonstrates how successful CNNs are in image classification tasks. Below is the output of the all of the code above:

```
Downloading data from https://s3.amazonaws.com/img-datasets/mnist.npz
11493376/11490434 [==============================] - 15s 1us/step
x_train shape: (60000, 28, 28, 1)
60000 train samples
10000 test samples
Train on 60000 samples, validate on 10000 samples
Epoch 1/12
60000/60000 [==============================] - 105s 2ms/step -
    loss: 0.2674 - acc: 0.9184 - val_loss: 0.0584 - val_acc:
    0.9809
Epoch 2/12
60000/60000 [==============================] - 106s 2ms/step -
    loss: 0.0893 - acc: 0.9734 - val_loss: 0.0444 - val_acc:
    0.9863
Epoch 3/12
60000/60000 [==============================] - 108s 2ms/step -
    loss: 0.0682 - acc: 0.9798 - val_loss: 0.0387 - val_acc:
    0.9864
Epoch 4/12
60000/60000 [==============================] - 109s 2ms/step -
    loss: 0.0565 - acc: 0.9835 - val_loss: 0.0365 - val_acc:
    0.9889
Epoch 5/12
60000/60000 [==============================] - 110s 2ms/step -
    loss: 0.0472 - acc: 0.9860 - val_loss: 0.0311 - val_acc:
    0.9899
Epoch 6/12
60000/60000 [==============================] - 110s 2ms/step -
    loss: 0.0418 - acc: 0.9878 - val_loss: 0.0343 - val_acc:
    0.9893
Epoch 7/12
```

```
60000/60000 [==============================] - 109s 2ms/step -
    loss: 0.0354 - acc: 0.9895 - val_loss: 0.0266 - val_acc:
    0.9918
Epoch 8/12
60000/60000 [==============================] - 107s 2ms/step -
    loss: 0.0341 - acc: 0.9897 - val_loss: 0.0306 - val_acc:
    0.9910
Epoch 9/12
60000/60000 [==============================] - 102s 2ms/step -
    loss: 0.0298 - acc: 0.9907 - val_loss: 0.0282 - val_acc:
    0.9915
Epoch 10/12
60000/60000 [==============================] - 103s 2ms/step -
    loss: 0.0290 - acc: 0.9911 - val_loss: 0.0273 - val_acc:
    0.9915
Epoch 11/12
60000/60000 [==============================] - 108s 2ms/step -
    loss: 0.0285 - acc: 0.9911 - val_loss: 0.0283 - val_acc:
    0.9915
Epoch 12/12
60000/60000 [==============================] - 118s 2ms/step -
    loss: 0.0253 - acc: 0.9920 - val_loss: 0.0249 - val_acc:
    0.9918
Test loss: 0.024864526777043875
Test accuracy: 0.9918
```

CNNs can be used in several different applications:

- **Identifying faces**. This application is particularly useful in image analysis cases. It works by first rejecting parts of the image that don't contain a face, which are processed in low resolution. It then focuses on the parts containing a face, and draws the perceived boundaries in high resolution for better accuracy.[21]

- **Computer vision (CV) in general**. Beyond face recognition, CNNs are applied in various other scenarios of computer vision. This has been a

---

[21] http://bit.ly/2o175Da.

hot topic for the past decade or so, and has yielded a variety of applications.[22]

- **Self-driving cars**. Since CV features heavily in self-driving cars, the CNN is often the AI tool of choice for this technology. Their versatility in the kind of inputs they accept, and the fact that they have been studied thoroughly, make them the go-to option for NVIDIA's self-driving car project, for example.[23]

- **NLP**. Due to their high speed and versatility, CNNs lend themselves well to NLP applications. The key here is to "translate" all the words into the corresponding *embeddings*, using specialized methods such as GloVe or word2vec. CNNs are optimal here since NLP models range from incredibly simple like a "bag of words" to computationally demanding like n-grams.[24]

Recurrent Neural Networks

Recurrent Neural Networks (RNNs) are an interesting type of DL network, widely used for NLP applications. They process data sequentially, resulting in an improved analysis of complex datasets, through the modeling of the temporal aspect of the data at hand. In a way, RNNs mimic human memory; this enables them to understand relationships among the data points like we do.

---

[22] http://bit.ly/2o5B63Y.

[23] http://bit.ly/2Hfxky2.

[24] http://bit.ly/21HCl4h.

Interestingly, RNNs can also be used for text-related artificial creativity. It's common for them to generate text that stylistically resembles some famous writer's prose or even poems, as we saw in chapter 2. Because of their popularity, RNNs have a few variants that are even more effective for the tasks in which they specialize.

RNN components

RNNs have "recurrent" as part of their name because they perform the same task for each element of a sequence, while the output depends on the previous computations. This takes the form of loops in an RNN's architecture, such as the one in Figure 14.

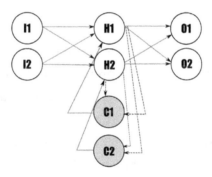

Figure 14. A graphical depiction of a quite rudimentary RNN. Note the recurrent nodes C1 and C2, corresponding to the hidden layer comprising nodes H1 and H2. Original image designer: Tiago Reul.

This architecture could make it possible for the network to consider an unlimited number of previous states of the data. In reality, though, it usually includes merely a few steps. This is enough to give the RNN system a sense of "memory," enabling it to see each data point within the context of the other data points preceding it.

Since the recurrent connections in an RNN are not always easy to depict or comprehend (particularly when trying to analyze its data flow), we often "unfold" them. This creates a more spread-out version of the same network, where the temporal aspect of the data is more apparent, as you can see in Figure 15. This process is sometimes referred to as "unrolling" or "unfolding".

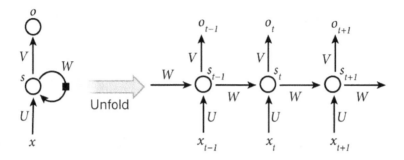

Figure 15. *Unfolding* an RNN, allowing us to better view its data flow. Image source: Nature

Data flow and functionality

The data in an RNN flows in loops, as the system gradually learns how each data point correlates with some of the previous ones. In this context, the hidden nodes of an RNN (which are often referred to as "states") are basically the memory of the system. As you would expect, these nodes have a non-linear activation function such as ReLU or tanh. The activation function of the final layer before the output usually has a softmax function, though, so as to approximate probabilities.

Contrary to a traditional DL system, which uses different weights at each layer, an RNN shares the same parameters across all steps. This is because it is basically performing the same task at every step, with the only difference being the inputs. This significantly decreases the total number of parameters it must learn, making the training phase significantly faster and computationally lighter.

Training process

When training an RNN, we employ many of the same principles as with other DL networks—with a key difference in the training algorithm (which is typically backpropagation). RNNs demand an algorithm that considers the number of steps we needed to traverse before reaching the node when calculating the gradient of the error of each output node. This variant of the training algorithm is called Backpropagation Through Time (BPTT). Because the gradient function is unstable as it goes through an RNN, the BPTT is not good at helping the RNN learn long-term dependencies among its data points. Fortunately, this issue is resolved using a specialized architecture called the LSTM, which we'll discuss in the next section.

RNN variants

When it comes to variants of RNNs, the ones that stand out are Bidirectional RNNs (as well as their "deep" version), LSTMs, and *GRUs*.

Bidirectional RNNs and their deeper counterparts

A bidirectional RNN is like an ensemble of two RNNs. The key difference between these two networks is that one of them considers previous data points, while the other looks at data points that follow. This way, the two of them together can have a more holistic view of the data at hand, since they know both what's before and what's after. A deep bidirectional RNN is like a regular bidirectional RNN, but with several layers for each time step. This enables a better prediction, but it requires a much larger dataset.

LSTMs and GRUs

Short for Long Short Term Memory, an LSTM network (or *cell*) is a very unique type of RNN that is widely used in NLP problems. It comprises four distinct

ANNs that work together to create a kind of memory that is not limited by the training algorithm (like it is in conventional RNNs). This is possible because LSTMs have an internal mechanism that allows them to selectively forget, and to combine different previous states, in a way that facilitates the mapping of long-term dependencies. Figure 16 demonstrates a standard LSTM *cell* with three gates (input, update, and output):

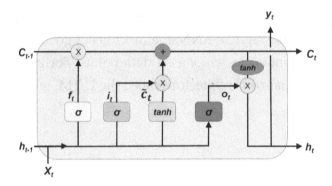

Figure 16. In the figure, the h variables represent short-term memories while the C variables represent long-term memories. The yellow gate is input, the green gate is update, and the red gate is output. Image source: https://bit.ly/2uCVBIL.

LSTMs are quite complex; as such, developers quickly sought a more straightforward version. This is where GRUs, or Gated Recurrent Units, come into play; a GRU is basically a lightweight LSTM. A GRU is an LSTM network with two gates—one for resetting, and one for updating previous states. The first gate determines how to best combine the new input with the previous memory, while the second gate specifies how much of the previous memory to hold onto.

RNNs in action

Here we provide an example of text classification using the LSTM variant of the RNN. The code is implemented in Python and Keras. The dataset we use is from the IMDB movie database; it is already available with the Keras' datasets module. The dataset includes IMDB's users' comments on movies and their associated sentiments. Our task is to classify comments as positive or negative sentiments—a binary classification task. The code below is taken from the official Keras repository.[25]

First, we begin by importing the relevant libraries, as usual. Notice that we also import the IMDB dataset from Keras' datasets module:

```
from __future__ import print_function
from keras.preprocessing import sequence
from keras.models import Sequential
from keras.layers import Dense, Embedding
from keras.layers import LSTM
from keras.datasets import imdb
```

Then, we set the maximum number of features to 20,000; the maximum number of words in a text to 80; and batch size to 32:

```
max_features = 20000
maxlen = 80
batch_size = 32
```

Next, we load the dataset into some variables, after splitting train and test sets:

```
(x_train, y_train), (x_test, y_test) =
    imdb.load_data(num_words=max_features)
```

We need to pad some text comments, as some of them are shorter than 80 words, and our model only accepts inputs of the same length. In short, padding works by adding a predefined word to the end of a sequence to make the sequence of the desired length. The code below pads the sequences:

```
x_train = sequence.pad_sequences(x_train, maxlen=maxlen)
x_test = sequence.pad_sequences(x_test, maxlen=maxlen)
```

---

[25] https://bit.ly/2FuKCog.

Now, we are all set to build our sequential model. First we add an embedding layer, and then we add an LSTM. Last, we add the dense layer for classification:

```
model = Sequential()
model.add(Embedding(max_features, 128))
model.add(LSTM(128, dropout=0.2, recurrent_dropout=0.2))
model.add(Dense(1, activation='sigmoid'))
```

After we build our model, we can now train on our train set. We use binary cross-entropy loss as our loss function, the Adam algorithm as our optimizer, and accuracy as our evaluation metric:

```
model.compile(loss='binary_crossentropy',
              optimizer='adam',
              metrics=['accuracy'])
```

It is time to train our model:

```
model.fit(x_train, y_train,
          batch_size=batch_size,
          epochs=10,
          validation_data=(x_test, y_test))
```

Last, we test the performance of our model using the test set:

```
score, acc = model.evaluate(x_test, y_test,
                            batch_size=batch_size)
print('Test score:', score)
print('Test accuracy:', acc)
```

The model achieves almost 82% accuracy on the test set after 10 epochs, which is a satisfactory result for such a simple model. The output of the code above is:

```
Train on 25000 samples, validate on 25000 samples
Epoch 1/10
25000/25000 [==============================] - 91s 4ms/step -
    loss: 0.4555 - acc: 0.7836 - val_loss: 0.3905 - val_acc:
    0.8279
Epoch 2/10
```

```
25000/25000 [==============================] - 90s 4ms/step -
    loss: 0.2941 - acc: 0.8813 - val_loss: 0.3796 - val_acc:
    0.8316
Epoch 3/10
25000/25000 [==============================] - 94s 4ms/step -
    loss: 0.2140 - acc: 0.9178 - val_loss: 0.4177 - val_acc:
    0.8311
Epoch 4/10
25000/25000 [==============================] - 96s 4ms/step -
    loss: 0.1565 - acc: 0.9416 - val_loss: 0.4811 - val_acc:
    0.8238
Epoch 5/10
25000/25000 [==============================] - 96s 4ms/step -
    loss: 0.1076 - acc: 0.9614 - val_loss: 0.6152 - val_acc:
    0.8150
Epoch 6/10
25000/25000 [==============================] - 92s 4ms/step -
    loss: 0.0786 - acc: 0.9727 - val_loss: 0.7031 - val_acc:
    0.8225
Epoch 7/10
25000/25000 [==============================] - 91s 4ms/step -
    loss: 0.0513 - acc: 0.9831 - val_loss: 0.7056 - val_acc:
    0.8166
Epoch 8/10
25000/25000 [==============================] - 91s 4ms/step -
    loss: 0.0423 - acc: 0.9865 - val_loss: 0.8886 - val_acc:
    0.8112
Epoch 9/10
25000/25000 [==============================] - 91s 4ms/step -
    loss: 0.0314 - acc: 0.9895 - val_loss: 0.8625 - val_acc:
    0.8140
Epoch 10/10
25000/25000 [==============================] - 91s 4ms/step -
    loss: 0.0255 - acc: 0.9920 - val_loss: 1.0046 - val_acc:
    0.8152
25000/25000 [==============================] - 14s 563us/step
Test score: 1.0045836124545335
Test accuracy: 0.8152
```

Before closing this chapter, we will bring to your attention several other advanced DL models (e.g. GANs), contained in appendices of this book. We strongly encourage you to read those appendices to learn more on DL models. After that, you can find many other useful resources to dig into the details of DL models.

RNNs are ideal tools to solve the following problems:

- **NLP.** As mentioned before, RNNs excel at working with natural language text. Tasks like predicting the next word or figuring out the general topic of a block of text are solved well by RNNs.

- **Text synthesis.** A particular NLP application that deserves its own bullet point is text synthesis. This involves creating new streams of words, which is an extension of the "predicting the next word" application. RNNs can create whole paragraphs of text, taking text prediction to a whole new level.

- **Automated translation.** This is a harder problem than it seems, since each language and dialect has its own intricacies (for instance, the order of words in constructing a sentence). To accurately translate something, a computer must process sentences as a whole—something that's made possible through an RNN model.

- **Image caption generation.** Although this is not entirely RNN-related, it is certainly a valid application. When combined with CNNs, RNNs can generate short descriptions of an image, perfect for captions. They can even evaluate and rank the most important parts of the image, from most to least relevant.

- **Speech recognition.** When the sound of someone talking is transformed into a digitized sound wave, it is not far-fetched to ask an RNN to understand the context of each sound bit. The next step is turning that into written text, which is quite challenging, but plausible using the same RNN technology.

Summary

- Convolutional Neural Networks (CNNs) and Recurrent Neural Networks (RNNs) are two of the most popular neural network architectures beyond ANNs. CNNs are very good at image related tasks like image recognition and image captioning and RNNs are quite efficient in sequential tasks like machine translation.

- CNNs achieve state-of-the-art performance on some computer vision tasks, and have even surpassed human performance.

- RNNs are very suitable for tasks that can be represented as sequences.

- There are many variants of RNNs. Two most popular are LSTMs and GRUs. LSTMs are comprised of four gates and GRUs are comprised of two gates. In this respect, GRUs are lightweight versions of LSTMs.

## CHAPTER 10

Building an Optimization Ensemble

Ensembles are generally useful when it comes to data science systems, since they combine the best features of various methods. Just as any machine is more than the sum of its parts, these complex ensembles perform better than their individual components. The goal of any ensemble is to produce a better result than you could with any one single method—though the result an ensemble produces is usually limited by the best-performing optimization method contained therein.

We'll examine how optimization ensembles work, how they can benefit from parallelization, and work through some examples using the PSO optimizer as well as combinations of PSO and Firefly. We'll close by discussing how all this fits within data science, as well as some useful considerations for optimization ensembles in general.

Optimization ensembles often go by the term "hybrid systems" when it comes to scientific literature. However, we prefer to avoid adding yet another term to the vast lexicon of data science when "ensemble" works well as a general descriptor plus it's the term most commonly used in the industry. So, if you come across the term "hybrid" in a paper, as in the case of a Simulated Annealing variant mentioned in Chapter 8, remember that they are referring to an ensemble system.

Optimization ensembles combine the performances of various optimization systems that tackle the same problem. These systems may be iterations of the same method, with different parameters and/or starting values, or they can comprise of different methods altogether.

Alternatively, optimization ensembles can exchange data from one optimizer to another, in an attempt to further improve accuracy of the results. Naturally, this approach requires a more in-depth understanding of the methods involved, as well as more fine-tuning each solution to the problem at hand. In this chapter we'll focus on the simpler ensemble described in the previous paragraph.

The role of parallelization in optimization ensembles

Parallelization is a key to creating ensembles, as it enables the optimization methods to work simultaneously. Much like big data modeling systems that use various machines (or components, like GPUs) to process data while simultaneously training a system, parallelized optimizers can train and seek the optimum solution at the same time, trying out different strategies. This can minimize the risk of getting trapped in a local optimum, or getting an inaccurate solution due to a sub-optimal configuration in the optimizer's parameter settings.

Parallelization therefore makes better use of available resources, saving us time and facilitating better results. Depending on the nature of a problem, some optimizers can be designed to focus on only one part of the problem, such as the rough optimization that takes place in the beginning, before zeroing in on the optimum solution. This may require some advanced programming, though, so we won't delve into it in this chapter.

Framework of a basic optimization ensemble

Let's now examine a basic optimization ensemble, comprising two optimizers working in parallel. Each system has different parameters, but they are both sharing the same fitness function (otherwise it wouldn't be an ensemble at all). Once they search for solutions, they compare their outputs. The solution that corresponds to a higher or lower value (depending on whether it is a maximization or a minimization problem) is selected as the output of the whole system (see Figure 17).

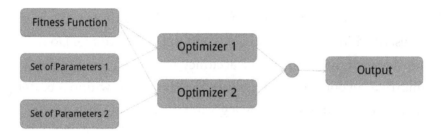

Figure 17. A diagram of a basic optimization ensemble. Note that the fitness function is the same in both, and that the optimizers' outputs are compared before a single output is yielded by the ensemble. In this diagram, the circle node signifies the merging of the two signals yielded by the two optimizers. This merging takes place using a basic operator like min() or max(), depending on the optimization mode we are using.

The key strength of this setup is that the two optimizers work simultaneously, so the whole system is quite fast. You can create an ensemble of more than two optimizers, each with its own set of parameters, all sharing the same fitness function—provided there are enough processing units to run them.

Note that if the optimizers used in the ensemble have significantly different running times, this will result in delays. This is because the ensemble wrapper function must wait for all the workers to finish, not being able to outpace its slowest optimizer.

Case study with PSO Systems in an ensemble

To make all this more concrete, let's consider a basic optimization ensemble consisting of three PSO systems, working to minimize a given function. These examples are based on a quad-core computer, so they are appropriate for a machine having at least this computing power. If you are using an older computer, you will need to adjust the number of workers to suit its specifications—otherwise you may experience delays when running the ensemble code.

For starters, let's get the PSO code in memory. The code for this is similar to what we described in Chapter 6, so we won't detail it here too. Do note the one minor improvement, made for better accuracy in the results: if the best solution doesn't improve beyond a given tolerance threshold (tol) within a buffer period, the maximum velocity diminishes by a given factor (in this case 0.618).

Next, we need to load the *Distributed* package from the Base package so that we can use parallelization:

```
using Distributed
```

Next, we need to add a few workers to apply parallelization:

```
addprocs(3)
```

We can verify that we now have 4 workers (one for each PSO system in the ensemble) as follows:

```
nprocs()
```

Even though we only need 3 workers for this example, we strongly recommended adding *all* the workers you will need for the *entire* project during this initialization phase. Otherwise, you risk serious confusion among the functions used by these workers.

Afterwards, we need to load a function called swi() to help us with sorting matrices, available in a custom script called SortWithIndexes.jl:

```
include("SortWithIndexes.jl")
```

Next, we need to define the fitness function (let's call it FF) for the optimizers, and we'll opt to minimize it:

```
@everywhere function FF(X::Array{Float64})
    return y = X[1]^2 + abs(X[2]) + sqrt(abs(X[3]*X[4])) + 1.0
end
```

For this function to be accessible to all the workers, it must be preceded by the *@everywhere* meta-command. The same prefix is added to the pso() function, implementing the PSO algorithm for each available worker, as well as in the swi() function for the matrix sorting process. If you bring additional workers onboard later, they will not have access to the FF function—until you run the previous code again. Similarly, if you plan to run different versions of an optimizer among these workers, it is best to activate each worker and run its corresponding optimizer code individually, without the @everywhere meta-command.

For the wrapper function driving the whole ensemble, we'll use the following code. It's basically a meta-PSO function, encompassing all the optimizers in the ensemble, through their corresponding workers:

```
function ppso(ff::Function, minimize::Bool = true, nv::Int64 = 4,
    ps::Int64 = 10*nv, ni::Int64 = 2000)
    np = nprocs()
    F = Any[ff for i = 1:np]
    Z = pmap(pso, F)
    G = Array{Float64}(undef, np)

    for i = 1:np
        G[i] = Z[i][2]
    end
```

```
        if minimize
            ind = indmin(G)
        else
            ind = indmax(G)
        end

        println(G)
        return Z[ind]

end
```

In this case we don't need to use the *@everywhere* meta-command, since the function doesn't need to run on every single worker. Also, the println() command is not entirely necessary, though it can be helpful if you'd like to see how the various members of the ensemble perform.

To run the PSO ensemble on the fitness function F, just type:

```
    ppso(FF, true, 4)
```

This ensemble's solution is very close to the global optima of [0, 0, 0, R] and [0, 0, R, 0] (where R is any real number), having a fitness value of 1.0. The solution found in this case is [-0.00527571, -1.66536e-6, 1.44652e-5, -3.29118e-6], corresponding to a fitness value of about 1.00008. This is quite close to the actual optimal value, even though the whole process of finding this solution was not noticeably slower than running a single PSO search.

Because of the default settings of the ppso() function, even if we typed ppso(FF), the ensemble would still work. Also remember that to use this function for a maximization problem, you must set the second parameter to "false" first:

```
    ppso(FF, false, 4)
```

Case study with PSO and Firefly ensemble

Let's now consider another basic optimization ensemble, this time involving two different optimizers: a PSO optimizer and a Firefly optimizer. (For a refresher on this optimization method, refer to the corresponding paragraph of Chapter 6). The objective in this case is again to minimize a given function. To make things more interesting, we'll have two optimizers for each algorithm, for a total of 4 workers.

In this example, we'll need the code for both PSO and Firefly. For the latter, we need to employ some auxiliary functions, all of which are contained in the corresponding notebook. For brevity's sake, we'll omit that code here. The Firefly optimization system is implemented using a function called ffo().

For the ensemble, we can use the wrapper function *co()*, which stands for "combined optimizer":

```
function co(ff::Function, minimize::Bool = true, nv::Int64 = 5)
    np = round(Int64, nprocs() / 2)  # number of processors for
     each optimizer
    N = 2*np
    F = Function[ff for i = 1:np]
    M = Bool[minimize for i = 1:np]
    NV = Int64[nv for i = 1:np]
    G = Array{Float64}(undef, N)
    X = pmap((ff, minimize, nv) -> ffo(ff, minimize, nv), F, M,
     NV)
    Y = pmap((ff, minimize, nv) -> pso(ff, minimize, nv), F, M,
     NV)
    Z = vcat(X, Y)

    for i = 1:N
        G[i] = Z[i][2]
    end

    if minimize
        ind = findmin(G)[2]
```

```
        else
            ind = findmax(G)[2]
        end

        println(G)
        return Z[ind]
    end
```

As in the previous example, we don't need to use the *@everywhere* meta-command for this function, since it doesn't need to run on every single worker. Remember, we only need the *@everywhere* meta-command if the code needs to run on every single worker, i.e. in parallel. Wrapper functions generally don't need that.

The println() command in the function is purely for educational purposes, allowing you to view the results of the various members of the ensemble. In this case, it's particularly interesting, as we have optimizers from two different families (the first two being PSO and last two being Firefly).

To test the whole thing on the fitness function F (defined previously), we just need to type:

```
co(F, true, 4)
```

This returns a solution very close to the global optimum, [-0.0103449, 6.77669e-8, -7.33842e-7, -7.93017e-10], corresponding to the fitness value of about 1.0001. The fitness values of the best solutions of the optimizers are: 1.01052, 1.00636, 1.0003, and 1.00011, respectively. Although the final result is not as accurate as the previous example's, it is quite good overall. Considering that the PSO systems didn't do so well in this problem, the ensemble still managed to perform well, thanks to the other two Firefly optimizers.

The co() function is versatile by design, in terms of the number of workers used. It basically allocates half the available workers to one optimizer, and the remaining workers to the other. You can experiment with it using different numbers of workers, particularly if you have enough processing units at your disposal.

How optimization ensembles fit into the data science pipeline

At this point you may be wondering how all this optimization ensemble stuff is relevant to the data science process. After all, you can get insights with more conventional methods such as basic machine learning system and statistical models, or through the deep learning systems we examined in the first part of the book. How do optimization ensembles improve upon these existing methodologies?

In short, most modern data science problems involve optimization in one way or another, and conventional optimizers just won't cut it. Older methods worked well for the simple problems they were built for. Just a few decades ago, analysts (with lots of patience and a knack for math) solved simple problems by hand. But data science is a huge realm with massive quantities of complex data, though, involving many dimensions and variables.

What's more, although the optimizers we studied may be able to handle these problems, oftentimes we don't have the time to fine-tune these systems. That's where optimization ensembles come in. From performing feature selection to optimizing the boundaries of parameters in a 1-class SVM for anomaly detection, optimization is essential to many data science projects.

More importantly, solving complex optimization problems efficiently through ensembles will give you a better perspective on problem-solving in data science.

Many available methods are already optimized, but sometimes you may need to break new ground, tackling a problem that hasn't been tackled before (at least, not in the open-source world). That's where experience with ensembles (and other topics just beyond the crash-course level) can come in handy, since not all problems can or should be solved with off-the-shelf methods. The scope of a good data scientist is no longer limited to traditional data science methods, expanding rapidly to include AI methods like optimization ensembles.

Ensemble tips

The optimization ensembles covered in this chapter may seem straightforward, but as usual, you must keep a few key things in mind. For example, you must ensure that the optimizers are set up properly, by configuring the corresponding parameters with values that make sense for the problem at hand. Otherwise, the results may not be that useful or there is going to be a lot of wasted computational resources (e.g. from delayed convergence).

Also, you are better off using optimizers you are quite comfortable with and that you understand well. This way, you can obtain good results from such a system, even if the optimizers you use are instances of the same algorithm. Besides, due to their stochastic nature, they are bound to yield different solutions anyway every time you run them, so putting them in an ensemble can definitely have some positive impact on the result of the optimization.

When building an optimization ensemble, pay attention to the computing power at your disposal. Julia can create as many workers as requested, but if the power of the workers exceeds the capacity of the processing threads available in your machine, the ensemble will not be efficient. Some threads will need to take on more tasks than others, leading to an imbalance of workload that is bound to delay the whole system. Remember, the workers may correspond to individual CPUs or GPUs when their number is small. If that number exceeds the total processing units accessible to Julia, though, there is bound to be an issue, even if it doesn't throw any errors or exceptions.

What's more, using an optimization ensemble does not guarantee that the solution will be a global optimum. Sometimes, even a group of ensembles can become trapped in local optima, yielding a sub-optimal solution at the end of the pipeline. Still, the chances of that are smaller when using an ensemble than when using a single optimizer.

Summary

- Optimization ensembles (also called "hybrid systems") utilize a combination of optimizers to tackle a given fitness function. Such an ensemble can produce a result at least as good as the result of its best-performing member.

- Optimization ensembles come in different forms. Simple ensembles run two (or more) optimizers in parallel on a given problem, and then compare their outputs. The optimizers can be of different algorithm families, though it's best to use algorithms with similar running times, to ensure efficiency.

- The coding in a basic optimization ensemble is quite straightforward. Use the *@everywhere* meta-command to make sure all the optimizer functions are available to all the workers in the ensemble.

- Understanding the ins and outs of optimization ensembles will help you hone your problem-solving skills, and empower you to tackle challenging and complex data science problems. Such problems may not be commonplace, but when they do arise, they are often critical to the project at hand.

• When working with optimization ensembles, remember to set the parameters properly and pay attention to the computing power available.

• The result of an optimization ensemble is not guaranteed to be a global optimum, but it is almost certainly better than the result of any one of its components alone.

## CHAPTER 11

Alternative AI Frameworks in Data Science

Since the inception of AI, a lot of efforts have been made to discover new techniques and approaches, contributing to the development of the discipline. Sometimes new advances are subtle variations on older ones; other times we abolish the older techniques and start from scratch. Although the literature on artificial intelligence rests upon the decades-long efforts of researchers and practitioners, the dynamics of change and improvement persist.

Here we'll mention some alternative AI frameworks that seem promising to us. In doing so, we hope not only to equip you with more problem-solving tools, but also to highlight this dynamic field's tremendous potential for improvement and change. The topics covered in the previous chapters cover the more popular AI frameworks. Becoming familiar with some alternative AI frameworks can help you explore the possibilities of future frontiers of the current research.

In this chapter we cover the three alternative frameworks that we believe will stand the test of time and be used into the future. The first of these is the Extreme Learning Machines, a family of network-based systems quite similar to the neural network ones we saw before, with a major difference regarding optimization of hidden layers. The second alternative framework is the Capsule Network, which is another invention of renowned AI expert Professor Geoffrey

Hinton. The final alternative we'll discuss is the Fuzzy Logic and Fuzzy Inference System, a framework developed by one of the people who put AI on the map, Professor Zadeh.

Extreme Learning Machines (ELMs)

You may recall from our discussion of Deep Learning that multi-layer feed forward networks comprise multiple layers connected to each other. The first layer is called the input layer, the last layer is the output layer, and between are the hidden layers. When we train a multi-layer feed forward network using backpropagation, we tune all the weights associated with the connections that are present between all the connected layers. Even if we start with a random initialization for the weights (as we usually do), in each iteration of the backpropagation algorithm, we update the weights accordingly. Remember that we use numerical approximation methods (like Gradient Descent, for instance) to implement backpropagation.

The central idea in ELMs is that only the weights of the output layers should be tuned; the weights of the hidden nodes should not be tuned. Before explaining ELMs in detail, let's first consider the goals of ELMs, to understand why we'd choose to not tune weights for the hidden nodes.

Motivation behind ELMs

When Frank Rosenblatt proposed the concept of a *perceptron* in 1958, he believed that *perceptrons* would one day enable a computer to "walk, talk, see, write, reproduce itself and be conscious of its existence."[26] Not long after that, though,

---

[26] http://en.wikipedia.org/wiki/Perceptron.

Minsky and Papert showed that *perceptrons* without hidden layers could not even handle a simple XOR problem.[27] However, AI researchers have realized that hidden layers are critical components of any neural network model. Furthermore, it is proven that sufficiently complex architectures of a neural network model with hidden layers can approximate any continuous function - known as the universal approximation! Since then, including hidden layers in a neural network model and tuning the parameters of the hidden layer became a major practice in the neural networks literature.

According to the opponents of the idea that the ultimate goal of any artificial neural network is to mimic the functioning of the biological brains, the ANNs should be designed in accordance with the findings of Neuroscience. A central tenet in ELM literature is also this idea. Because, we know that biological brains and especially the human brains are excellent at learning new things. But the structure of the biological brain seems in sharp contrast with the notion that the hidden layers should be tuned. In short, the neurons in biological brains form layered structures as ANNs mimic. However, it sounds naive to expect that any single connection between two neurons in our brains adjust to every observation we encounter in our lives. Indeed, recent findings in neuroscience confirm this idea.[28] Hence, proponents of ELMs argue that in order for the ANNs to confirm with the workings of the biological brain, the hidden nodes of the ANNs should not be tuned.

---

[27] Minsky M, Papert S. Perceptrons: an introduction to computational geometry. Cambridge: MIT Press; 1969.

[28] Sosulski DL, Bloom ML, Cutforth T, Axel R, Datta SR. Distinct representations of olfactory information in different cortical centres. Nature. 2011;472:213–6; Eliasmith C, Stewart TC, Choo X, Bekolay T, DeWolf T, Tang Y, Rasmussen D. A large-scale model of the functioning brain. Science. 2012;338:1202–5; Barak O, Rigotti M, Fusi S. The sparseness of mixed selectivity neurons controls the generalization–discrimination trade-off. J Neurosci. 2013;33(9):3844–56; Rigotti M, Barak O, Warden MR, Wang X-J, Daw ND, Miller EK, Fusi S. The importance of mixed selectivity in complex cognitive tasks. Nature. 2013;497:585–90.

Architectures of ELMs

The simplest Extreme Learning Machine is a feed-forward network with a single hidden layer; it's actually quite similar to a single-layer perceptron model. However, if we use different ELMs for each layer, it is easy to extend this single-hidden-layer architecture to multi-hidden-layer feed forward networks.

Let's start with a single-hidden-layer feed forward architecture. Figure 18 shows the basic architecture of an ELM, with an input layer, a hidden layer, and an output layer. As mentioned earlier, the architecture is comparable to that of a single-layer feed forward network. The difference is that when we optimize single-layer ELM, we do not tune the weights of the hidden layer. We just tune the output layer's weights.

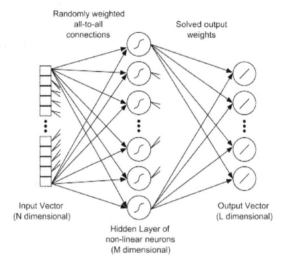

Figure 18: The basic architecture of an extreme learning machine. SOURCE: Tissera, Migel D., and Mark D. McDonnell. "Deep extreme learning machines: supervised autoencoding architecture for classification." Neurocomputing 174 (2016): 42-49.

The building blocks of multi-hidden-layer feed forward ELMs are simply single-hidden-layer feed forward ELMs. In this case, we combine different single-layer elements stack by stack. In effect, each hidden layer is just another ELM. This essentially makes a multi-layer ELM an ensemble of ELMs, though a bit more sophisticated than those we saw in the previous chapter.

Figure 19 demonstrates a multi-hidden-layer feed forward ELM as a combination of two single layer ELMs. In this multi-hidden-layer architecture, consider each hidden layer representative of an operation or role. For example, each single ELM layer could deal with compression, feature learning, clustering, regression, or classification, which are the basic operations or roles of any ELM.

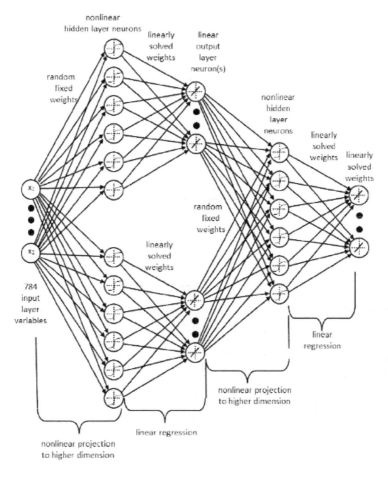

Figure 19: The basic architecture of a multi-hidden layer extreme learning machine. SOURCE: Tissera, Migel D., and Mark D. McDonnell. "Deep extreme learning machines: supervised autoencoding architecture for classification." Neurocomputing 174 (2016): 42-49.

In another alternative architecture for multi-hidden-layer ELMs, a hidden node itself can be a sub-network formed by several nodes. As a result, some local parts of a single ELM can contain multi-hidden layers.

Again, the basic tenet of ELMs is that hidden layers should not be tuned. Although randomly assigning values to the weights of hidden layers is an option, it's not the only available option. Alternatively, a hidden node in any given layer might be a linear transformation of the nodes in the previous layer. As a result, some nodes are randomly generated and some are not, but none of them are tuned.[29] One last thing to note before closing the discussion of ELMs is that ELMs can be combined with other learning models. The output of the other models can be fed into the ELMs, or the output of the ELMs can be fed into other models as inputs. This is referred to as stacked models, and is another form of ensembles.[30]

Capsule Networks (CapsNets)

The Capsule Network (or CapsNet) is a new type of neural network model, proposed in 2017 by Professor Geoffrey Hinton and some of his students. It shows incredible promise for computer vision tasks in particular. As we discussed earlier, CNNs are usually sufficient to solve these problems, but CNNs do have some drawbacks. CapsNets might be able to cover some of the CNNs' blind spots.

---

[29] Moreover, another kind of randomness can also be integrated into the ELMs. In this case, input layers to hidden nodes can be fully or partially randomly connected according to different continuous probability distribution function.

[30] A great resource for the properties of the ELMs can be found here: https://bit.ly/2JoHhcg.

Although the idea of a basic architectural element "capsule" is not new, the model developed by Hinton and his students is truly novel. Until their work, nobody had known how to train a model built upon capsules. Professor Hinton and his colleagues also proposed a new method to train these methods, called "dynamic routing between capsules."

Motivations behind CapsNets

The Convolutional Neural Networks have proven to be remarkably successful at computer vision tasks, including image recognition and object detection. However, the orientation of and spatial relationships between these components are not important to CNNs. Factors such as view angle, perspective, and the relative positions of objects are not considered. For example, in Figure 20, a CNN would find the two face-like shapes are almost identical. Of course, it is obvious to us humans that the right figure is not a face at all, even if some modern art enthusiasts would still see a face in that image.

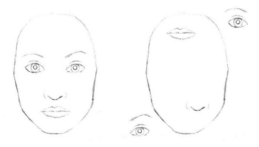

Figure 20: These two images would both be considered faces by a CNN. Source: https://bit.ly/2NTVsJB.

To mitigate these drawbacks of CNNs, Hinton argued that we should come up with new types of network structures that resemble the workings of our brains as they are great at handling the aforementioned drawbacks of the CNNs. According to Hinton, our brains do something called "inverse graphics" such that when we see something in the world with our eyes, our brains deconstruct a hierarchical representation of the information, trying to match it with learned relationships and patterns that are already stored in our brains. Those concepts in our brains do not depend on the perspective or view angle of the objects. To classify images and recognize objects more accurately, the key is to preserve hierarchical "pose" relationships between different components of the objects.

CapsNets incorporate these relative relationships between objects by representing them as 4-dimensional pose matrices. For a capsule network, the same objects in the upper and lower rows of Figure 21 would be interpreted as identical.

Figure 21: For a capsule network, the same objects in the upper row and the below row are considered the same. Source: https://bit.ly/2NgLHEg.

The CapsNet created by Hinton and his students decreased the error rate of the previous state-of-the-art model by 45% in a 3-dimensional image recognition task! Moreover, CapsNet achieves its performance using only a fraction of the previous model's training set. In these regards, CapsNets do a good job of acting more like our human brains do. Next, let's briefly look at the architecture of CapsNets.

Architecture of CapsNets

CapsNet includes six layers. The first three are the encoders, and the last three are the decoders:

1. Convolutional layer
2. PrimaryCaps layer
3. DigitCaps layer
4. Fully connected layer
5. Fully connected layer
6. Fully connected layer

Figure 22 illustrates the first three layers of encoders:

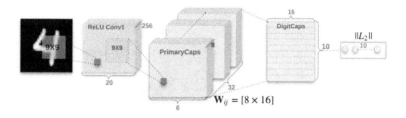

Figure 22: The encoders (first three layers) in a CapsNet. Source: https://bit.ly/2yyTvP2.

We've already discussed the convolutional layer. It's the next two layers that use capsules. A *capsule* is a set of neurons that individually turns on for various properties of a type of object, such as position, size, and hue. Formally, a capsule is a set of neurons that collectively produce an activity vector with one element for each neuron to hold that neuron's instantiation value, such as hue.[31] In other words, a capsule is a nested set of neural layers (much like a sophisticated ensemble of sorts). In the neural networks we examined in previous chapters, we were adding layers on top of each other. In CapsNets, though, we add more layers *inside* a single layer. Effectively, inside a capsule, the state of the neurons capture the properties (like size, position, or hue) of one object inside an image.[32]

---

[31] https://bit.ly/2PP3NQ0.

[32] Other minor differences between CNNs and CapsNets exist, but are not as significant. Consult Footnote 22 for a link with further reading.

After encoders, the decoding layers come in. Figure 23 illustrates these last three layers, which are all fully-connected that work as decoders.

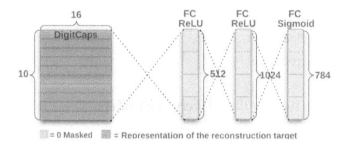

Figure 23: The decoders (the last three layers) in a CapsNet. Source: https://bit.ly/2yyTvP2.

Now, how do we train CapsNets, given that backpropagation doesn't apply?

Dynamic routing between capsules

CapsNets learn by using a dynamic routing algorithm between capsules, which we will examine here in some detail. Table 1 shows the steps of the algorithm, as explained in the original paper by Hinton et al.[33] We will omit the detailed explanation of the algorithm to the readers, but will point out that the novel part of the algorithm occurs at line 7, where the weights are updated. At this line, each low-level capsule consults each high-level capsule, examines the input for each, and then updates the corresponding weight.

The updating formula, which is used in the optimization when updating the weights, states that the new weight value equals the old value plus the dot product of the current output of capsule j, and the input to this capsule from a lower-level capsule i. The lower-level capsule will send its output to the higher-level capsule where the higher-level capsule's output is similar. This similarity is

---

captured by the dot product. Notice that the algorithm repeats r times, where r is the number of routing iterations.

Procedure 1 Routing algorithm.

1: **procedure** ROUTING($\hat{\boldsymbol{u}}_{j|i}, r, l$)
2:     for all capsule i in layer l and capsule j in layer $(l+1)$: $b_{ij} \leftarrow 0$.
3:     **for** r iterations **do**
4:         for all capsule i in layer l: $\mathbf{c}_i \leftarrow \texttt{softmax}(\mathbf{b}_i)$ $\triangleright$ softmax computes Eq. 3
5:         for all capsule j in layer $(l+1)$: $\mathbf{s}_j \leftarrow \sum_i c_{ij}\hat{\mathbf{u}}_{j|i}$
6:         for all capsule j in layer $(l+1)$: $\mathbf{v}_j \leftarrow \texttt{squash}(\mathbf{s}_j)$ $\triangleright$ squash computes Eq. 1
7:         for all capsule i in layer l and capsule j in layer $(l+1)$: $b_{ij} \leftarrow b_{ij} + \hat{\mathbf{u}}_{j|i}.\mathbf{v}_j$
        return $\mathbf{v}_j$

Table 1: A dynamic routing algorithm. Source: https://arxiv.org/abs/1710.09829

If you want to delve deeper into CapsNets, start with the papers written by Hinton and his students, already mentioned in this section. Research to further investigate CapsNets has already begun. In the future, we'll likely see remarkable performances from these models in some challenging tasks.

Fuzzy logic and fuzzy inference systems

As we saw briefly in Chapter 2, Fuzzy Inference Systems (FIS) are systems based on Fuzzy Logic (FL), and are designed to perform predictive analytics in a comprehensive manner. The approach they use is somewhat different from other AI systems, as they generate rules during their training, and apply them when given unknown data. Since they use membership functions instead of probability estimates, the approach employed in this whole process is *possibilistic*. We'll explain this concept shortly.

Fuzzy sets

At the core of FL is the concept of "fuzzy sets", which are entities that don't have crisp boundaries and therefore lend themselves to a potentially infinite number of grades. Just as our eyes cannot identify one exact point where the color green ends and the color yellow begins, a fuzzy set A has different levels of membership for the various data points that may have A as an attribute.

For instance, if you want to know how far away a place is, you could represent its distance as a series of fuzzy sets. Each fuzzy set would correspond to a certain threshold or level of distance—like walking distance, a bus ride, or a day-trip; or the more abstract terms close, medium, and far). Each one of these levels may be expressed as a mathematical function (represented as the letter μ), referring to different parts of the distance variable (e.g. far). These functions almost always overlap in some way, and are often triangular or trapezoidal in shape, for lower computational cost (see Figure 24).

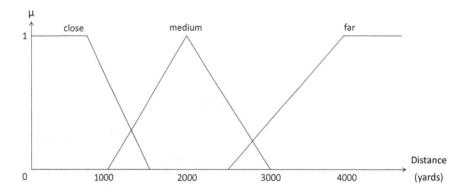

Figure 24. A fuzzy representation of distance. Note the three different levels used (close, medium, and far), corresponding to three overlapping fuzzy sets, expressed as the corresponding membership functions.

It is important to note that these levels are often selected in a way that makes sense to us, since they tend to correspond to how we express these quantities in our own natural language. The inherent ambiguity of these expressions is perfectly acceptable, however, since it captures the uncertainty that is always involved in these scenarios (e.g. "far" may mean different things to different people). This uncertainty is modeled through the values of the membership functions of these levels.

FIS functionality and fuzzy rules

A FIS basically examines the data it is given, expresses it in a series of fuzzy rules, and creates a model synthesizing the most useful of these rules. It works very much like a decision tree, though more sophisticated and better-performing. The rules that a FIS ends up using are also easy to plot, and can be insightful on their own.

Making use of a FIS involves applying the best rules it has found during its training phase to generate a set of predictions, usually accompanied by a confidence metric. Even if a lot of ambiguity is involved in these rules, the end-result is always unambiguous (crisp) since after the defuzzification process, everything becomes clear-cut. The whole process can be summarized in Figure 25.

Figure 25. FIS functionality diagram. Note that the fuzzy representation of the data involved is in this form only within the system itself, as the outputs (prediction and rules) are always crisp.

The aforementioned rules involve connecting two or more fuzzy sets in an intuitive way that takes the form of an IF-THEN clause. A fuzzy rule, then, is a systematic way to link one or more fuzzy sets to a decision (which is usually crisp). For example, depending on how you wanted to traverse a certain city distance over time, such as walk, take a bike or bus, or call a Lyft or Uber cab, you could model the problem using the following rules (among others):

```
IF {distance = close} THEN {walk}
IF {time = limited} THEN {call a cab}
IF {distance = medium} AND {time = enough} THEN {take a bike /
    bus}
IF {distance = medium} AND {time = plenty} THEN {walk}
IF {distance = high} AND {time = plenty} THEN {take a bike / bus}
IF {distance = high} AND {time = enough} THEN {call a cab}
```

These rules may be expressed in a matrix format as well, for convenience:

Distance / Time	Limited	Enough	Plenty
Close	Walk OR Call a cab	Walk	Walk
Medium	Call a cab	Take a bike / bus	Walk
Far	Call a cab	Call a cab	Take a bike / bus

Although a well-designed FIS should keep the overlap of rules to a minimum, it is still possible. Also, it is possible that certain scenarios are not covered by a rule—though such cases are best avoided, unless you are *certain* that they would never occur in practice.

Naturally, when you apply these rules, you'll be using specific numbers, so they'll manifest in a more mathematical way. In other words, while the different rules may appear very general, they become quite specific when applied. Say, for example, you have an engagement 1200 yards away and you have 30 minutes to get there. We may construct the following membership mappings:

Set A / Set B	Limited: 0.20	Enough: 0.90	Plenty: 0.10
Close: 0.25	Walk: 0.55 Cab: 0.35	Walk: 0.90	Walk: 0.40
Medium: 0.15	Cab: 0.25	Bike / Bus: 0.70	Walk: 0.25
Far: 0.00	Cab: 0.00	Cab: 0.00	Bike / Bus: 0.00

The values for each means of transport are derived from the rule application process, which involves predefined mathematical operators like min, mean, or max, that apply to the membership functions for the variables involved.

The combining of the above values into a "crisp" number (i.e. one that has no membership values attached to it) for each transport option is done through the defuzzification method. This is usually performed using a method like "moment of area," corresponding to the center point of the polygon deriving from the merged membership functions). So, we may end up with something like the following:

Prediction Option	Membership value
Walk	0.80
Take a bike / bus	0.55
Call a Lyft / Uber cab	0.10

From this, we can predict with reasonable confidence that, in this particular situation, it is best to walk. Note, however, that for a different city, the mappings would be different, and the results would likely differ too.

Fortunately, plenty of packages (in most data science languages) enable the use of FL and FIS in various applications. Below are some of the most interesting ones.

Python

scikit-fuzzy: an extension of the well-known scikit learn package, focusing on the core FL operations. More at https://pypi.org/project/scikit-fuzzy.

fuzzywuzzy: an interesting package focusing on string matching using FL. More at https://github.com/seatgeek/fuzzywuzzy.

pyfuzzy: an older package covering FL operations. More at http://pyfuzzy.sourceforge.net/ .

Peach: possibly the most relevant package out there on this topic, covering various AI systems used in data science as predictive analytics systems. More at https://code.google.com/archive/p/peach/.

Julia

Fuzzy.jl: a compact package containing various tools for both basic FL as well as FIS. This is an unofficial package that's still under development. More at https://github.com/phelipe/Fuzzy.jl.

Some fuzzy logic tips

Fuzzy Logic is ideal in cases where the uncertainty inherent in the phenomena modeled is better described by language than by math. Sometimes mathematical functions may be suitable to represent the memberships like the Gaussian function, so FL could be considered a flexible extension of conventional modeling methods. FL shines where there exists knowledge (perhaps from a domain expert) that can be utilized to create fuzzy rules, or when you wish to extend an expert system model. In this case, FL is like an intermediary between human knowledge and machine-structured information.

The refinement of membership function in a FIS is often achieved via an optimization method. However, care must be taken so that the system doesn't overfit, since the possibility of creating an overly-sophisticated model is present in this kind of AI too. One of the most robust systems under the FIS umbrella is ANFIS, which makes use of an ANN architecture to optimize the membership functions involved.

Although FL is great at modeling uncertainty and building robust predictive models based on a variety of datasets (through a FIS), it is not so practical when it comes to high-dimensionality datasets, due to the explosion of potential rules. In cases like these we often sacrifice interpretability for performance (for example, by reducing dimensionality). However, if you have a relatively small feature selection method at your disposal, you may want to use that first; such a dimensionality reduction method preserves the comprehensiveness of the original feature set as no meta-features are created (as in the case of PCA, for example).

Finally, the number of levels used for each variable can be either set manually or derived automatically. Not all variables need to be modeled in the three-level fashion of the examples shown here.

Summary

- Extreme Learning Machines (ELMs) are among the most popular alternative frameworks in data science.

- The basic tenet of ELMs is that hidden layers should not be tuned at all.

- Although ELMs can be used individually, they can also be integrated with other learning models.

- Capsule Networks (CapsNets) are a new type of neural network that aim to better capture the hierarchical representations of objects.

- The optimization algorithm used in the CapsNets is called Dynamic Routing Between Capsules.

- CapsNets are good at identifying the perspectives and view angle in images; these are main weak points of the alternative CNNs.

- A *Fuzzy Inference System (FIS)* examines the data it is given, expresses it in a series of fuzzy rules, and creates a model comprising the most useful of these rules.

- The rules a FIS ends up using are easy to plot, and can be insightful on their own.

- Although Fuzzy Logic (FL) is great at modeling uncertainty and building robust predictive models based on a variety of datasets (through a FIS), it is not so practical when it comes to high-dimensionality datasets, due to the explosion of potential rules that can be derived.

## CHAPTER 12

Next Steps

We've covered many things in this book. Most of the book is dedicated to the popular and useful approaches that have broad applicability in today's AI challenges. We discussed basic deep learning concepts and models, as well as several programming libraries that prove to be very convenient in implementing deep learning models. The basic optimization algorithm that is mostly used in deep learning today is backpropagation, and we've provided several examples that use this optimization method.

However, modern tasks involving AI are rather huge; backpropagation is only applicable to the functions that are differentiable. Prominent AI researcher François Chollet put it this way:[34]

"Backprop is a centralized answer, that only applies to differentiable functions where "control" means adjusting some parameters and where the optimization objective is already known. Its range of applicability is minuscule."

With this in mind, we provided other optimization algorithms (such as Particle Swarm Optimization, Genetic Algorithms, and Simulated Annealing) to cover the optimization possibilities of many of the AI tasks, as well as several other applications in both the industry and in scientific research. And finally, we presented a general picture of alternative AI frameworks, so that you can have a complete grasp of artificial intelligence in today's data science world.

---

[34] https://bit.ly/2wsdhIC.

In this final chapter of the book, we'll cover the "next steps" required to advance beyond this book and enhance your understanding of the data science domain. First, we briefly discuss big data, which has become essentially inescapable. After that, we outline some of the prominent specialization areas of data science today. We hope that this discussion will provide you with some perspectives regarding the broad areas that can be involved in your future projects. Finally, we list some useful, publicly-available datasets that you can use to practice and to research.

Big data

The term "Big Data" is probably one of the most commonly used terms in computer science today. Although the definition of the term is somewhat blurry (as the name includes the very subjective term "big"), we can succinctly define it as the amount of data that is big enough so that an average personal computer is unable to process it." By this definition, the term "big" refers to terabytes, petabytes, or even exabytes of data (to give you a sense of proportion, if you gather all the data a person would normally access throughout his or her lifetime, it's unlikely to reach over 1 exabyte).

To further narrow the definition, consider the *four Vs* described by IBM.[35] Big data is constantly increasing in *volume*, arriving in growing *velocity*, sourced by ever-increasing *variety* and with uncertainty around *veracity*. These so-called *four Vs—volume, velocity, variety, and veracity*—are among the most important characteristics of big data in today's highly-connected digital world.

---

[35] We want to warn our readers that they will find all sorts of additional "Vs" in the literature and on the Internet. Here we use IBM's definition as it is brief and concise. Source: https://ibm.co/2AFln5v.

Why is big data important? The answer to this question lies within just two statements:

1. Big data enables us to get more complete answers to our questions because it includes a lot of information.
2. We rely on these answers with more confidence, because as the amount of data increases, our confidence level usually goes up.

The successes of the deep learning algorithms that we covered in the previous chapters are also related to big data. The two main reasons that deep learning has been so successful are the advances in the computational power of modern computers, and the huge amount of data that is available to use.

To work with huge amounts of data, two recent technologies are quite important; we dedicate the rest of the big data discussion to these technologies. One of them is *Hadoop* and the other one is *Spark,* which are both open-source projects created by Apache Foundation. We encourage you to learn more about them, as they are especially useful in tackling huge amounts of data.

Hadoop

If we want to store data just for backup purposes, then the amount of data may not be a first-order concern for a data scientist. More often than not, though, we want to analyze that data, gleaning useful insights from the information that is hidden there. A distributed data storage technology called Hadoop was developed just to meet this need.

Hadoop (usually referred to as "Hadoop cluster") has four key components: Commons, YARN, *HDFS*, and MapReduce. Commons is Hadoop's utilities structure, and YARN is a tool for resourcing and scheduling in Hadoop. HDFS is the abbreviation for Hadoop Distributed File System; this is where the data is actually stored. MapReduce is a data processing tool for distributed systems. Figure 26 illustrates the components of Hadoop in a simple way.

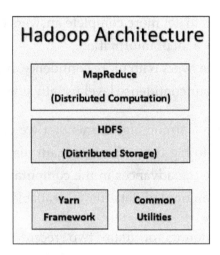

Figure 26: The basic components of Hadoop. Hadoop comprises Commons, YARN, HDFS and MapReduce. Source: https://bit.ly/2NTVBg7.

As a data scientist, you probably use a larger set of tools than just the above four. You use these tools because they make your life easier. They usually abstract away the architectural and administrative parts of working in a Hadoop cluster. The basic thing a data scientist want to experience with data that is stored on a Hadoop cluster is probably querying the data as if querying a single machine relational database management system rather than administering a Hadoop cluster.

To this end, you can use *Hive* and its querying language *HiveQL*. Using *HiveQL*, one can forget about the distributed nature of the data and write queries as if all the data is on a single machine. Due to the huge volumes of data on HDFS, though, the *HiveQL* queries usually take more time than traditional SQL queries! Other tools (like Presto) provide faster access to the data on HDFS, but they are usually more computationally expensive, and their requirements are more demanding.

Apache Spark

So far we've covered how to store and access big data in a clustered and distributed manner. Since the ultimate objective of a data scientist is to build analytical models upon that data, we need some other technology to conveniently work with the data stored on HDFS.

Apache Spark is one of the most commonly-used technologies that provides distributed computing. Spark simplifies some common tasks including resource scheduling, job execution, and reliable communication between nodes of a cluster. As of 2018, Spark supports five programming languages: Scala, Python, Julia, R, and Java.

Spark uses a data representation called the *Resilient Distributed Dataset (RDD)*, which is very similar to the dataframes in Python, Julia, and R. RDD supports distributed computing by working on multiple machines, where it uses the memories of all these distributed computers in a cluster. Once an RDD is in place, you can use Spark to interact with this distributed data as if the data were on the memory of a single machine. This way, Apache Spark isolates the distributed nature of the computing infrastructure for the user, which is very convenient when working on a data science task. Figure 27 depicts the basic architecture of Apache Spark.

The Python example below illustrates how a few lines of code in Apache Spark can easily count words in a document stored on HDFS:

```
text_file = sc.textFile("hdfs://...")
counts = text_file.flatMap(lambda line: line.split(" ")) \
        .map(lambda word: (word, 1)) \
        .reduceByKey(lambda a, b: a + b)
counts.saveAsTextFile("hdfs://...")
```

The first line reads distributed data from an HDFS. The flatMap() function separates each word in the text file. The map() function combines each word with 1 as a key-value tuple. The reduceByKey() function adds up the numbers for the same keys (which are words, in this example). The last line just saves the results—that's it!

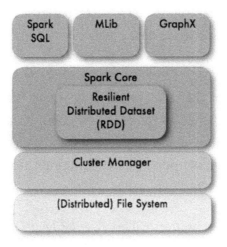

Figure 27: The architecture of Apache Spark. It includes a distributed file system (like HDFS), a cluster manager, a Spark Core (RDD), and high-level APIs (like MLib, Spark SQL, and GraphX). Source: https://bit.ly/2JqBWks.

Specializations in data science

Lately data science has become a broad discipline, so specializing in a specific domain is usually a necessity rather than a luxury. Here we discuss some different niche areas within data science, in hopes of helping you decide which area you are most interested in.

Data Engineering

Earlier in this chapter, we talked about big data and some related technologies. We pointed out that large amounts of data require special treatment, in terms of storing and computing environments. Today, managing huge amounts of data is a time-consuming task that demands a specialization related to systems administration and database management.

Data engineers are responsible for gathering, storing, and securing data. They are also the ones who manage the infrastructure of a data science or machine learning pipeline within a company or organization. In this respect, data engineering is related more to system administration than to data science. However, for those of you with interest in working with these aspects of technology, data engineering positions might be the most relevant.

Natural Language Processing

Natural Language Processing (NLP) is a specific area within artificial intelligence that focuses on the tasks related to human languages. These tasks include text summarization, topic modeling, language modeling, machine translation, text categorization, sentiment analysis, and many more. The technology that Google Translate incorporates is just one commonplace application of NLP. Not all NLP-related tasks fall under the AI umbrella, since certain structures (like knowledge-representation systems), although useful to NLP, don't share any of the traits of modern AI systems.

NLP inherits many concepts and insights from linguistics, combining these with statistical machine learning methods to solve the challenges of understanding human language. This field is on the leading edge of such technologies as sequence-to-sequence translation between languages, chatbots, search engines, and machine translation systems.

Computer Vision

Computer vision is another AI domain that aims to make machines understand the visual aspects of the world we all live in. The models and methods used in computer vision process the digital images or videos that are provided to them. Image recognition, object detection, and object tracking are only a small subset of the tasks tackled by computer vision today.

Some fantastic applications of computer vision expertise are motion recognition, augmented reality, autonomous cars, robotics, image restoration, and image generation. Also, computer vision has a lot to offer in *Augmented Reality* applications, where virtual reality objects are overlaid on real world views. Because of all that, we believe that computer vision will continue to be one of the most promising areas of study within artificial intelligence and data science.

Internet of Things

This term (often abbreviated IoT) refers to the fact that in today's world, billions of gadgets and all kinds of machines are constantly connected to the Internet (chances are that you are reading an electronic version of this book through one of them!). As computers go from small to tiny (e.g. Raspberry Pi), they can fit into more and more commonplace devices, leading to an explosion of affordable "smart" gadgets. The data that all these connected devices generate is tremendous, and provides a very vast playing field for data science. The big data infrastructure required to store and process this huge quantity of data necessitates big data expertise.

Furthermore, analyzing this much data is also a special focus of data science. Anomaly detection and predictive maintenance are just two examples of the applications of data science within the IoT. With the continuing increase of the number of devices that are connected to each other and to the Internet, IoT will become one of the core areas of study in data science.

Biostatistics and Healthcare

Another field that increasingly depends upon data science is biostatistics. From predicting diseases to research on genomics, data science is a cornerstone of healthcare. Related to the IoT, wearable health gadgets are another area of expertise for data scientists. Considering the crucial importance of health care in people's lives, we believe that biostatistics and healthcare are among the most promising areas of specialization in data science.

Social Sciences

This field is too large to begin to dissect in detail, but it is clear that analyzing people (their habits, their spending, or their relationships, for instance) on a large scale demands sophisticated methods. Time series methods in particular have huge applicability in social sciences, especially given modern advances in computational power and the availability of data.

Obviously, this is not an exhaustive list of niches within data science. These are simply highlights that are relatively popular nowadays. Furthermore, many interdisciplinary areas (such as robotics, for instance) can include different components of artificial intelligence (like computer vision and NLP). Consider, for example, how Augmented Reality combines computer vision with many other processes as we briefly saw earlier.

It takes a lot of practice to become an expert in just about anything, including any one of these data science sub-domains. Of course, you won't be able to practice without access to useful tools and datasets. To this end, in the next section, we provide some resources you may find useful.

Publicly available datasets

Studying artificial intelligence science requires reliable (and, ideally, interesting) data. Since the topics in this book cover mostly supervised learning methods, the data those methods need should be labeled beforehand. The data should be accompanied with the true classes or the true values of the target variables. However, labeling a dataset is not a trivial task. As such, we usually use a publicly-available dataset that is already labeled. In the previous chapters of this book, we provided examples using a couple of synthetic datasets that we prepared for you, as well as some public datasets that are popular in literature.

One of the great resources that includes many useful datasets is *Kaggle,* a website that focuses on data science competitions. These competitions gather thousands of teams around the world to compete against each other to solve a specific data science task. Kaggle also hosts a lot of useful datasets.[36] Moreover, participating in Kaggle competitions is also an effective way to practice your data science skills, particularly those related to data modeling. You can also analyze the kernels that are provided by participants, as they contain many useful insights.

In addition to Kaggle's datasets, here we provide a list of useful datasets that are publicly available. The list covers datasets that are commonly used in computer vision, natural language processing, speech recognition, and time series analysis.

---

[36] https://www.kaggle.com/.

Computer vision

- **MNIST:** This is very popular dataset comprises 25x25 centered handwritten digits. It includes 60,000 training examples and 10,000 test examples. Visit https://bit.ly/1REjJgL.

- **CIFAR 10 and CIFAR 100:** The CIFAR-10 dataset consists of 60,000 32x32 color images in 10 classes, with 6,000 images per class. There are 50,000 training images and 10,000 test images. The CIFAR-100 dataset is just like the CIFAR-10, except it has 100 classes containing 600 images each. There are 500 training images and 100 testing images per class. The 100 classes in the CIFAR-100 are grouped into 20 super classes. See https://bit.ly/1QZAvsv.

- **ImageNet:** This is a very popular dataset of images with 1,000 categories. Visit https://bit.ly/2Lk69DC.

- **Open Images:** This is a dataset of around 9 million images that have been annotated (by Google) with image-level labels and object bounding boxes. The 4th version training set contains 14.6 million bounding boxes for 600 object classes on 1.74 million images, making it the largest existing dataset with object location annotations. See https://bit.ly/2JqJ5Bf.

Natural language

- **WikiText:** The WikiText language modeling dataset is a collection of over 100 million tokens extracted from the set of verified Good and Featured articles on Wikipedia. Visit https://bit.ly/2NSPI2J.

- **Quora Question Pairs:** This comprises over 400,000 lines of potential question duplicate pairs. Each line contains IDs for each question in the pair, the full text for each question, and a binary value that indicates whether the line truly contains a duplicate pair. See https://bit.ly/2upwz0x.

- **SQuAD:** Stanford Question Answering Dataset (SQuAD) is a reading comprehension dataset, consisting of questions (posed by crowdworkers) on a set of Wikipedia articles. The answer to every question is a part of the text from the corresponding reading passage. The question might also be unanswerable by just the corresponding article. Version 2 contains 100,000 questions, and can be viewed at https://bit.ly/2v0G8At.

- **Billion Words:** This large, general-purpose language modeling dataset is found at https://bit.ly/2Ll43Dy.

- **Common Crawl:** This contains petabytes of data collected over 8 years of web crawling. The corpus contains raw web page data, metadata extracts, and text extracts. See https://bit.ly/2NQjZzv.

- **Stanford Sentiment Treebank:** This is a common sentiment dataset, found at https://stanford.io/2uwa8qz.

Speech in English

- **2000 HUB5 English Transcripts:** This was developed by the Linguistic Data Consortium (LDC). It comprises transcripts of 40 English telephone conversations used in the 2000 HUB5 evaluation, which was sponsored by NIST (National Institute of Standards and Technology). Visit https://bit.ly/2JrtkKn.

- **LibriSpeech:** This corpus contains approximately 1,000 hours of 16kHz read English speech, prepared by Vassil Panayotov with the assistance of Daniel Povey. The data is derived from read audiobooks from the LibriVox project, and has been carefully segmented and aligned. See https://bit.ly/2zJnjJC.

- **TIMIT:** This contains broadband recordings of 630 speakers of eight major dialects of American English, each reading ten phonetically rich sentences. Visit https://bit.ly/2zJni8w.

Social sciences and time series

- **World Bank:** The World Bank is an international institution that collects and publishes data about economic and social development, as well as financial indicators. These datasets are useful especially for data science practitioners in social sciences, and for those who are interested in time series analysis. See https://bit.ly/2yUZmdS.

- **IMF:** The International Monetary Fund is an international institution that focuses on monetary stability. Its datasets consist of financial and monetary indices that are useful in time series analysis. Visit https://bit.ly/2FqDyNr.

Summary

- Big data is critical to artificial intelligence and modern data science. Enormous amounts of data are constantly generated by our highly-connected digital world. This data demands special technologies for storage and analysis. Hadoop and Spark, which are both projects of Apache Foundation, are two useful technologies for big data.

- There are many specialization areas of data science; it is common for data scientists to specialize in one (or a few) areas.

- One of the most important resources of data is found at *www.kaggle.com*. Kaggle hosts data science competitions and provides many datasets.

- There are some publicly-available datasets that are useful for practicing data science. You will enhance your understanding of data science and gain expertise by building models on top of these datasets. Most of the datasets listed already have some benchmark scores, so that you can compare the performances of your models with the benchmarks.

Closing Thoughts

Our hope is that you have received a very broad yet practical perspective on AI from this book. Since this field changes so rapidly, with advances in AI coming from both older and newer players around the world, keep your eyes out for the upcoming second edition!

What will not require any updates for a second edition, however, is the general framework of thinking about data science and AI from a practitioner's lens. After all, no matter how much the tools change, core methodologies are bound to remain relevant. We made a deliberate effort to focus on principles and approaches, without getting lost in the hype that surrounds this field.

We hope that you will use this book as a basis to further your understanding and aptitude in AI, so that you make good use of this promising technology. You don't need to be an AI expert to benefit from AI systems— especially when it comes to data science related projects. However, if you really want to maximize your benefit, we recommend dedicating at least 6 months of your time to serious study of this field. No book can replace a hands-on course with individualized instruction; such classes can be found at universities or other specialized learning institutions. After all, data science AI is a field that involves problem-solving and creativity, rather than the mechanical application of some "recipe" geared towards a particular programming language.

Speaking of programming, with the rapid growth of *functional programming* languages these days, we thought it would be useful to expose you to both a conventional OOP language (like Python) and a newer one (like Julia), which is geared more towards the functional paradigm. This way, whatever happens with the constantly changing programming landscape in the AI field, you'll be ready.

Thank you for taking the time to read this book. We hope you have found it useful and we look forward to contributing to this field through additional materials on its various relevant topics. We believe that curiosity is the main driver of the successes of the AI and data science today. If this book has provoked your curiosity about this field, then we count ourselves successful.

Glossary

A

Activation function: see *transfer function*.

Agents: also known as bots or intelligent agents, they are autonomous software programs that aim to "sense" through sensors and "act" through actuators, according to their target function. Often they are leveraged as a way to mimic human behavior as assistants in a variety of functions. There are five classes of agents according to Russell & Norvig: simple reflex agents, model-based reflex agents, goal-based agents, utility-based agents, and learning agents.

Algorithm: a step-by-step procedure for calculations and logical operations. In an AI setting, algorithms can be designed to facilitate machine learning and acquire knowledge by themselves, rather than relying on hard-coded rules.

Amalgamation: the process of putting a system into a single file, that can be ported to different computer platforms. The executable file that it yields, has a very limited number of dependencies (sometimes it's even self-sufficient), making it a flexible option for deploying a system.

Apache Spark: a unified analytics engine for large scale data processing. It is designed for distributed computing and supports distributed data storage like HDFS.

API (Application Programming Interface): a set of definition, protocols, tools, and routines, for interacting with a program, usually via the Internet. APIs are essential for linking programming languages to various frameworks like *deep learning* ones.

Architecture (of a Deep Learning system): the way the *neurons* of an *artificial neural network* are organized and the connections among them.

Artificial creativity: a novel methodology of AI whereby the AI system emulates human creativity in a variety of domains, including painting, poetry, music composition, and even problem-solving. Artificial creativity has an important role in data science also.

Artificial Intelligence (AI): a field of computer science dealing with the emulation of human intelligence using computer systems and its applications on a variety of domains. AI's application on data science is noteworthy and an important factor in the field, since the 2000s.

Artificial Neural Network (ANN): a graph-based artificial intelligence system, implementing the universal approximator idea. Although ANNs have started as a *machine learning* system, focusing on *predictive analytics*, they have expanded over the years to include a large variety of tasks. ANNs comprise of a series of nodes called *neurons*, which are organized in layers. The first layer corresponds to all the inputs, the final layer to all the outputs, and the intermediary layers to a series of *meta-features* the ANN creates, each having a corresponding weight. ANNs are stochastic in nature so every time they are trained over a set of data, the weights are noticeably different.

Augmented Reality (AR): a sub-field / application of *artificial intelligence* that delves in the combination of real world data, such as a video feed of what's in front of you, with computer-generated data stream, related to what is observed, in a single video feed. The augmented view can have an informative role or increase functionality in some other way. AR requires specialized hardware as well as software combining *computer vision* and other processes.

Autoencoder: an *artificial neural network* system designed to represent codings in a very efficient manner. Autoencoders are a popular *artificial intelligence* system that are used for *dimensionality reduction,* as well as a few other *unsupervised learning* applications.

Automated Machine Learning (AutoML): Google's AI project responsible for creating an AI that designs and implements its own AI, for computer vision purposes.

B

Backpropagation: a very popular *training* algorithm for *deep learning* systems and *artificial neural networks* in general. It involves moving the errors of the network backwards (towards the inputs), and changing the *weights* of the various *neurons* based on the partial derivatives of the *error function*, as well as their location on the network.

Big data: an area of computer science that is interested in the efficient processing and storage of very large amounts of data. Although defining the term changes person to person, one can succinctly define big data as the amount of data that is big enough so that an average personal computer is unable to process it.

Binarization: the data engineering process of turning a discreet variable into a binary *feature*.

C

Chatbot: an artificial intelligence system that emulates a person on a chat application. A chatbot takes as its inputs text, processes it in an efficient manner, and yields a reply in text format. A chatbot may also carry out simple tasks, based on its inputs and it can reply with a question in order to clarify the objective involved.

Chromosome: a potential solution to a problem, modeled using *Genetic Algorithms*.

Classification: a very popular *data science* methodology, under the *predictive analytics* umbrella. Classification aims to solve the problem of assigning a *label* (aka class) to a data point, based on pre-existing knowledge of categorized data, available in the *training set*.

Classifier: a *predictive analytics* system geared towards *classification* problems.

Cloud (computing): a model that enables easy, on-demand access to a network of shareable computing resources that can be configured and customized to the application at hand. The cloud is a very popular resource in large-scale *data analytics* and a common resource for *data science* applications.

Clustering: a *data science methodology* involving finding groups in a given *dataset*, usually using the distances among the data points as a similarity metric.

Cognitive computing (CC): a set of processes and methods that involves self-learning systems that use data mining, pattern recognition, natural language processing and speech recognition to mimic the way the human brain works. CC can be viewed as a special kind of *artificial intelligence*.

Computational Intelligence (CI): a subclass of artificial intelligence, geared towards computational problems, such as *optimization*.

Computer cluster: a collection of computers sharing resources and working together, usually as a single machine. Computer clusters are very useful for tackling big data problems in-house, though more often than not, are found in data centers, forming public computer *clouds*.

Computer Vision: an application of *artificial intelligence*, where a computer is able to discern a variety of visual inputs and effectively "see" a lot of different real-world objects in real-time. Computer vision is an essential component of all modern robotics systems.

Context: a characteristic of an *NDArray*, whereby the data is assigned to a particular processing unit (a GPU), to better utilize the available computing resources.

Convolutional Neural Networks (CNNs or ConvNets): a type of *deep learning ANN* that involves a series of specialized layers when processing the (usually high-dimensionality) data, for various *predictive analytics* applications (mainly *classification*). CNNs are closely tied to *computer vision* and *Natural Language Processing*.

Crossover: a process in the *Genetic Algorithms* framework, whereby two *chromosomes* merge resulting to a new pair of chromosomes, that are candidates for the next *generation*.

D

Data analytics: a general term to describe the field involving data analysis as its main component. Data analytics is more general than *data science*, although the two terms are often used interchangeably.

Data engineering: the part of the *data science pipeline* where data is acquired, cleaned, and processed, so that it is ready to be used in a *data model*. Most *artificial intelligence* systems handle a large part of the data engineering once they are given the data that we want them to model.

Data exploration: the part of the *data science pipeline* where the various variables are examined using statistics and *data visualization*, in order to understand it better and work out the best ways to tackle it in the stages that follow.

Data model: a data science module processing and/or predicting some piece of information, using existing data, after the latter has been pre-processed and made ready for this task. Data models add value and are comprised of non-trivial procedures. In AI, data models are usually sophisticated systems making use of several data-driven processes under the hood.

Data science: the interdisciplinary field undertaking data analytics work on all kinds of data, with a focus on big data, for the purpose of mining insights and/or building data products.

Data visualization: the process of creating visuals based on the original data, or the data stemming from the *data model* built using the original data.

Dataset: the data available to be used in a *data analytics* project, in the form of a table or a matrix. A dataset may need some work before it is ready for being used in a data model, though in many *artificial intelligence* models, you can use it as is.

Data structure: a collection of data points in a structured form, used in programming as well as various parts of the *data science pipeline*.

Deep belief network (DBN): several *Restricted Bolzmann Machines* stacked together in a *deep learning* network fashion.

Deep Learning (DL): an *artificial intelligence* methodology, employing large *artificial neural networks*, to tackle very complex problems. DL systems require a lot of data in order to yield a real advantage in terms of performance.

Dimensionality reduction: the process of reducing the number of *features* in a *dataset*, usually through the merging of the original features in a more compact form (*feature fusion*), or through the discarding of the less information-rich features (*feature selection*). Dimensionality reduction can be accomplished in many ways, usually using some specialized *artificial intelligence* systems such as *autoencoders* and *Restricted Bolzmann Machines*.

Docker: a container software geared towards creating programming environments on a computer, containing all the required programs and data, so that an application can run on that computer smoothly, even if it was developed on a machine with a completely different configuration.

E

Elitism: an aspect of *Genetic Algorithms*, according to which, the best performing *chromosome* or chromosomes are preserved as they are, for the next *generation*.

Ensemble: "The process by which multiple models, such as classifiers or experts, are strategically generated and combined to solve a particular computational intelligence problem. Ensemble learning is primarily used to improve the (classification, prediction, function approximation, etc.) performance of a model, or reduce the likelihood of an unfortunate selection of a poor one." (Dr. Robi Polikar). Ensembles may also involve AI systems too, such as optimizers, in order to attain a better performance than a single such system.

Embedding: a low-dimensional representation of a given set of data. Embeddings are quite common in deep learning systems, particularly in *autoencoders* and in representing words in *Natural Language Processing* tasks.

Epoch: an iteration in the *training* phase of an *Artificial Neural Network*.

Error function: the function used for assessing the deviation of predicted values of a *machine learning* model from the actual values (*target* variable). In *artificial neural network* models, the error function needs to be continuous.

ETL (Extract, Transform and Load): a process in all data related pipelines, having to do with pulling data out of the source systems (usually databases) and placing it into a data warehouse or a data governance system. ETL is an important part of data acquisition, preceding any data modeling efforts.

Extreme Learning Machines (ELMs): a relatively new type of *artificial neural networks* that are very fast to train and exhibit decent performance in *predictive analytics* problems. Their key characteristics is that most of the connections have random weights, apart from those of the last *layer* (outputs), which are optimized during the training process.

F

Feature: a processed variable capable of being used in a *data science* model. Features are generally the columns of a *dataset*.

Feature engineering: the process of creating new features, either directly from the data available, or via the processing of existing features. Feature engineering is part of *data engineering*, in the data science process.

Feature fusion: see *fusion*.

Feature selection: the data science process according to which the dimensionality of a dataset is reduced through the selection of the most promising features and the discarding of the less promising ones. How promising a feature is depends on how well it can help predict the target variable and is related to how information-rich it is.

Feed-forward network: see *Multi-Layer Perceptron*.

Filter: a process in convolutional neural networks whereby features are created from an image by scanning it through a moving window (e.g. a 3x3 matrix).

Fitness function: an essential part of most *artificial intelligence* systems, particularly *optimization* related ones. It depicts how close the system is getting to the desired outcome and helps it adjust its course accordingly. In most AI systems the fitness function represents an error or some form of cost, which needs to be minimized, though in the general case it can be anything and depending on the problem, it may need to be maximized.

Framework: a set of tools and processes for developing a certain system, testing it, and deploying it. Most AI systems today are created using a framework. A framework is usually accompanied by a library/package in the programming languages it supports. In the *deep learning* case, for example, a framework can be a programming suite like *MXNet*, that enables a variety of DL related processes and classes to be utilized.

Fusion: usually used in conjunction with *feature* (feature fusion), this relates to the merging of a set of features into a single meta-feature that encapsulates all, or at least most, of the information in these features. This is a popular method of dimensionality reduction and it is an integral part of every *deep learning* system.

Fuzzy Inference System (FIS): an AI system based on *Fuzzy Logic*, geared towards making predictions using inference rules. A FIS is quite useful particularly when *interpretability* is a concern. However, it is limited to lower dimensionality datasets.

Fuzzy Logic: a term coined by Lotfi Aliasker Zadeh in 1965, referring to a different way of processing information which, unlike classical logic, also involves partial truths (instead of just the conventional black-and-white logical paradigm). Fuzzy logic uses degrees of truth as a mathematical model of vagueness and allows for all intermediate possibilities between digital values of YES and NO, much like how a human will assess the nature of a situation in full color and multi-polar fashion, rather than a bi-polar, monochrome way. Fuzzy logic is a well-established part of *artificial intelligence*.

G

Gene: an element of a *chromosome*, in a *Genetic Algorithms optimization model*. Genes are coded as bits and they represent a characteristic, referred to as a trait.

Generalization: a key characteristic of a *data science* model, where the system is able to handle data beyond its *training set* in a reliable way. A proxy to good generalization is similar performance between the training set and a testing set, as well as consistency among different training-testing set partitions of the whole *dataset*.

Generation: an iteration in the *Genetic Algorithms framework*.

Generative Adversarial Networks (GANs): a family of AI systems, each of which comprises two ANNs, one geared towards learning and one geared towards "breaking" the first ANN, by creating data that makes the first ANN get its predictions wrong. As a GAN is trained, each one of its components becomes better at its task, resulting in a highly effective AI system that can yield good generalization, even with a limited amount of data.

Genetic Algorithms (GAs): a family of *optimization* algorithms resembling the process of gene selection, combining, and mutation. They are well-suited for problems involving discreet variables, though they can be applied to continuous variables also. GAs are a well-established *artificial intelligence* methodology that finds many applications in *data science*, such as *feature selection*.

Genetic Programming (GP): an *artificial intelligence* methodology based on *genetic algorithms*, but geared towards finding an optimal mathematical function, to approximate a mapping of a particular variable.

Genome: the set of all the *chromosome* data in a *Genetic Algorithms* system. Genome and *population* are often used interchangeably in this context.

Gluon: a component of the *MXNet deep learning* framework, acting as an interface for the framework's various functions.

GPU (Graphics Processing Unit): a specialized component of a computer's hardware, designed for processing data related to the computer's display such as image-like data. GPUs can be leveraged to obtain additional computing power for resource-demanding tasks, such as AI systems, as in the case of *Deep Learning*.

Graph: a kind of dimensionless structure that is an abstraction of the objects involved in a process as well as their relationships (connections). It is characterized by nodes and arcs, representing the objects and the connections respectively. The latter also carry other characteristics too, such as weights, corresponding to the strength of each connection.

Graph analytics: a *data science* methodology making use of *Graph* Theory to tackle problems through the analysis of the relationships among the entities involved.

GRU (Gated Recurrent Units): a simpler version of an *LTSM* network.

H

Hadoop: a distributed data storage technology developed by Apache Foundation.

HDFS: abbreviation for *Hadoop* Distributed File System, a framework for storing and accessing data over a *computer cluster*, in an effective and efficient manner.

Heuristic: an empirical metric or function that aims to provide some useful tool or *insight*, to facilitate a method or project of *data science* or *artificial intelligence*.

Hive: an open source project of Apache Foundation. It is software that facilitates reading, writing, and managing large datasets residing in distributed storage using a variant of SQL called HiveQL.

HiveQL: query language of *Hive*.

I

IDE (Integrated Development Environment): a system designed for facilitating the creation and running of scripts as well as their debugging. *Jupyter* is a popular IDE for data science applications.

Interpretability: the ability to more thoroughly understand a *data model*'s outputs and derive how they relate to its inputs (*features*). Lack of interpretability is an issue for *deep learning* systems.

J

Julia: a modern programming language of the *functional programming paradigm*, comprising characteristics for both high-level and low-level languages. Its ease of use, high speed, scalability, and sufficient amount of packages, make it a robust language well-suited for *data science*. Recently v. 1.0 of the language was released, making it officially production-ready.

Jupyter: a popular browser-based *IDE* for various *data science* languages, such as Python and *Julia*.

K

Kaggle: a web site that hosts data science competitions and provides many useful datasets.

Keras: is a very popular high level deep learning API that can run on top of TensofFlow, CNTK, and Theano.

Kohonen's Maps: see *Self-organizing Maps*.

L

Layer: a set of *neurons* in an artificial neural network. Inner layers are usually referred to as hidden layers and consist mainly of *meta-features* created by the system.

Logistic function: see *sigmoid function*.

LTSM (Long Short Term Memory) network: a kind of *Recurrent Neural Network* that specializes in long-term dependencies among the data points. Comprising of four distinct *artificial neural networks*, an LTSM network is ideal of *natural language processing* applications.

M

Machine Learning (ML): a set of algorithms and programs that aim to process data without relying on statistical methods. ML is generally faster and some methods of it are significantly more accurate than the corresponding statistical ones, while the assumptions they make about the data are fewer. There is a noticeable overlap between ML and *artificial intelligence* systems designed for data science.

Mapping: the process of connecting a variable or a set of variables, to a variable we are trying to predict (aka target variable). Mappings can be analytical using a mathematical function, or not, such as employing a set of rules, or a network of functions, as in the case of an *artificial neural network*. Mappings are inherent in every *data model*.

Meta-features (aka super features or synthetic features): high quality features that encapsulate larger amounts of information, usually represented in a series of conventional features. Meta-features are either synthesized in an *artificial intelligence* system, or created through *dimensionality reduction*.

Methodology: a set of methods and the theory behind those methods, for solving a particular kind of problem in a certain field. Methodologies of *data science* include *classification*, *regression*, etc. while for *artificial intelligence*, we have methodologies like *deep learning*, *autoencoders*, etc.

Model Maintenance: the process of updating or even upgrading a *data model*, as new data becomes available or as the assumptions of the problem change.

Multi-Layer Perceptron (MLP): a *deep learning* system that comprises of a series of *layers* of *neurons*, much like a normal *ANN*, but larger. It is often referred to as a *feed-forward network* and it's the first system in the deep learning family to have been developed.

MLPs are great for various standard *data science* problems, such as *classification* and *regression*.

Mutation: a process in the *Genetic Algorithms* framework, according to which a random *gene* changes its value at random, with a given probability.

MXNet: a *deep learning* framework developed by Apache. MXNet is linked to Amazon, although it can run on any *cloud computing* service. Its main API is called Gluon and it's part of the main package of MXNet. There are several such packages in different programming languages, each one an *API* for that language. MXNet can support more programming languages than any other *AI* framework.

N

Natural Language Processing (NLP): a *text analytics* methodology focusing on categorizing the various parts of speech for a more in-depth analysis of the text involved.

Narrow AI: see *weak AI*.

NDArray: a data structure that is prominent in the *MXNet framework*. NDArrays are flexible like conventional data arrays, but also allow for *context* in the data stored in them, for more efficient processing of it.

Network: a collection of nodes, forming a data structure often used in *AI* systems. In computer science, networks are what are known as *graphs* in mathematics.

Neuron: a fundamental component of an artificial neural networks, usually representing an input (*feature*), a *meta-feature*, or an output. Neurons in a network-based *AI* system are organized in *layers*.

O

Objective function: see *fitness function*.

Optimization: an artificial intelligence process, aimed at finding the best value of a function (usually referred to as the *fitness function*) given a set of restrictions. Optimization is key in all modern *data science* systems. Although there are deterministic optimization algorithms out there, most of the modern algorithms are *stochastic*.

Optimizer: an *artificial intelligence* system designed to perform *optimization*.

Overfitting: the case whereby a model is too specialized to a particular dataset. Its main characteristic is great performance for the training set and poor performance for any other dataset. Overfitting is a characteristic of an overly complex model.

P

Package: a set of programs designed for a specific set of related tasks, sharing the same data structures, and freely available to the users of a given programming language. Packages may require other packages in order to function, which are called dependencies. Once installed, the package can be imported in the programming language and used in scripts.

Parallelizable: an attribute of many *systems* and *algorithms*, whereby different parts of them can be split among various CPUs or GPUs, working in parallel. This brings about a boost in performance that is often essential for AI processes. A parallelizable system is also more easily scalable.

Particle Swarm Optimization (PSO): a fundamental *optimization* algorithm, with a number of variants. Some claim that all *swarm intelligence* optimizers are based on PSO, since it is the simplest optimization algorithm of this category. PSO is geared towards continuous variables, though there is a variant of it for discrete ones. PSO has a variety of applications in all sorts of problems, involving a large number of variables (very large search space).

Perceptron: a rudimentary AI model and a fundamental component of an *artificial neural network*. When it comes to *classification*, a single perceptron can only handle very simple problems as it fails to generalize non-linear class boundaries.

Personally Identifiable Information (PII): information that can be used to pinpoint a particular individual, thereby violating his/her privacy. PII is an important ethical concern in data science and may not be so easy to tackle, since it often relies on combinations of variables.

Pipeline: also known as *workflow*, it is a conceptual process involving a variety of steps, each one of which can comprise of several other processes. A pipeline is essential for organizing the tasks needed to perform any complex procedure (often non-linear) and is very applicable in *data science* (this application is known as the data science pipeline).

Population: the totality of the elements involved in an optimization system, involving a number of solutions used at the same time. In some systems it is referred to as a swarm. Alternatively, the totality of the data describing a given phenomenon. Since this is often not available to the data scientist, samples of it are used instead.

Possibilistic modeling: a particular modelling paradigm sometimes used in *artificial intelligence* systems, making use of membership functions instead of probabilities, in order to model uncertainty in *Fuzzy Logic*.

Predictive analytics: a set of methodologies of *data science*, related to the prediction of certain variables. It includes a variety of techniques such as *classification, regression, time-series analysis,* and more. Predictive analytics are a key part of *data science*.

Pruning: the process of cleaning up code so that unwanted solutions can be eliminated. However, with this process, the number of decisions that can be made by machines is restricted.

Python: a widely used object-oriented programming language, typically used for *data science*, as well as *artificial intelligence* applications geared towards *data analytics*.

Q

Quantum computing: a new computing paradigm which leverages quantum effects and the use of *qubits*, for carrying out computing tasks potentially faster. Not all problems can be solved efficiently with quantum computing, but it is believed that *artificial intelligence* has a lot to benefit from it.

Qubits: short for quantum bits, a new kind of information unit, in the *quantum computing* paradigm. Unlike conventional bits, which can be either 0 or 1 only, qubits can take 0, 1, and both at the same time (leveraging the superposition concept from Quantum Physics).

R

Recurrent neural network (RNN): a *deep learning* network which employs a non-sequential flow in the data they process, resulting in an improved analysis of complex datasets, through the modeling of the temporal aspect of the data at hand. RNNs are ideal for *natural language processing* applications, as well as speech analysis projects.

Regression: a very popular *data science* methodology, under the *predictive analytics* umbrella. Classification aims to solve the problem of predicting the values of a continuous variable corresponding to a set of inputs, based on pre-existing knowledge of similar data, available in the *training set*.

Regressor: a *predictive analytics* system geared towards *regression* problems.

Reinforcement learning: a type of *machine learning* in which machines are "taught" to achieve their target function through a process of experimentation and reward. The machine receives positive reinforcement when its processes produce the desired result and negative reinforcement when they do not.

ReLU function: a minimalistic *transfer function* used in *deep learning*. It is defined as $f(x) = max(w*x+b, 0)$ and takes values between 0 and infinity. Being computationally cheaper and sparser than other transfer functions, it is sometimes preferred when creating a deep learning network.

Resilient Distributed Dataset (RDD): the data representation of Apache Spark that supports distributed computing.

Restricted Bolzmann Machine (RBM): a type of *artificial neural network*, geared towards learning the probability distributions of a set of features, in order to reconstruct them using a small set of meta-features. RBMs are similar to *autoencoders* in the sense that they too are often used for *dimensionality reduction*, though RBMs are used in other contexts, such as *predictive analytics*.

S

Sample: a limited portion of the data available, useful for building a model, and (ideally) representative of the population it belongs to.

Sampling: the process of acquiring a *sample* of a *population* using a specialized technique. Sampling is very important to be done properly, to ensure that the resulting sample is representative of the *population* studied. Sampling needs to be random and unbiased.

Scala: a functional programming language, very similar to Java, that is used in data science. The *big data* framework *Spark* is based on Scala.

Selection: a process of figuring out which *chromosomes* get to cross over, in the *Genetic Algorithms framework*. Selection is a stochastic process related to the *fitness* of the chromosomes involved.

Self-organizing Maps (SOMs): a special kind of *artificial neural network*, able to represent a feature space on a 2-dimensional plane, without the need of a *target variable*. In *data science*, SOMs are useful for *data visualization* and *data exploration*.

Sentiment analysis: a *natural language processing* method involving the *classification* of a text into a predefined sentiment, or the figuring out of a numeric value that represents the sentiment polarity (how positive or how negative the overall sentiment is).

Sigmoid function: a mathematical function of the form $f(x) = 1 / (1 + exp(-(w^*x + b)))$. Sigmoids are used in various *artificial neural networks*, such as *Deep Learning* networks, as *transfer functions*. Sigmoid takes values between 0 and 1, not inclusive. This is sometimes referred to as the *logistic function* as it features in logistic regression.

Simulated Annealing (SA): an *optimization* method in the nature inspired family of algorithms, based on the annealing process of liquids. SA is ideal for complex search spaces and it is very robust against local optima. A classical application of SA is the *Traveling Salesman Problem*.

Softmax function: a transfer function sometimes used in a deep learning network. It is a simpler version of the *sigmoid function,* where the bias parameter (b) is missing from the equation. Softmax takes values between 0 and 1, not inclusive.

Spark: see Apache Spark.

Stochastic: something that is probabilistic in nature. That is, not deterministic. Stochastic processes are common in most *artificial intelligence* systems and other advanced *machine learning* systems.

Strong AI: an area of AI development that is working toward the goal of making AI systems that are as useful and skilled as the human mind. It is often referred to as Artificial General Intelligence (AGI).

Supervised learning: a set of *data science methodologies* where there is a *target variable* that needs to be predicted. The main parts of supervised learning are classification, regression, and reinforcement learning.

Swarm: a set of potential solutions, evolving through a *swarm intelligence* framework. In the general case of different *optimization* systems, a swarm is referred to as *population.*

Swarm intelligence: a concept based on the idea that when individual agents come together, the interactions between them lead to the emergence of a more 'intelligent' collective behavior – such as a swarm of bees. Swarm intelligence is an essential part of modern optimization methods, such as *particle swarm optimization* and it is *stochastic* by nature.

T

Tanh function: the hyperbolic tangent function. It is of the same family as the sigmoid and it is sometimes used as a *transfer function* for *deep learning* networks. It is defined as f(x) = (exp(x) - exp(-x)) / (exp(x) + exp(-x)) and takes values between -1 and 1, not inclusive.

Target variable: the variable of a *dataset* that is the target of a *predictive analytics* system, such as a *classification* or a *regression* system.

Tensor Processing Unit (TPU): a special type of proprietary processor designed by Google in 2016 to accelerate the training of the neural network models implemented in the TensorFlow framework.

TensorFlow: a deep learning and high performance numerical computation library. Initiated by Google and improved by a very large open source community, TensorFlow is by far the most popular deep learning framework today.

Testing set: the part of the *dataset* that is used for testing a *predictive analytics* model after it has been trained and before it is deployed. The testing set usually corresponds to a small portion of the original *dataset*.

Training algorithm: the algorithm used for training a deep learning system (or a predictive analytics model in general). It entails figuring out which *nodes* to keep and what weights their connections have, so as to obtain a good *generalization* for the problem at hand. Back-propagation is an established training algorithm, suitable for various kinds of *artificial neural networks*, including deep learning systems.

Training set: the part of the *dataset* that is used for training a *predictive analytics* model before it is tested and deployed. The training set usually corresponds to the largest portion of the original *dataset*.

Trait: a characteristic of a problem, expressed as a *gene*, in the *Genetic Algorithms framework*.

Transfer function: a component of an *artificial neural network*, corresponding to the function applied on the output of a *neuron* before it is transmitted to the next *layer*. A typical example is the *sigmoid function*, though *ReLU* is often used in practice too. Transfer functions are sometimes referred to as *activation functions*.

Transfer learning: a *machine learning methodology* where a model trained for a task is reused in a second task without retraining. Taking the outputs of the pre-trained model as input to another model, this methodology tries to increase the performance of the second model as well as to reduce the training time.

Traveling Salesman Problem (TSP): a classical problem in *graph analytics*, whereby we opt to find the quickest path. That is, the one with the smallest overall cost in terms of time or distance, from one node of the *graph* to itself, after passing through all the other nodes once. TSP is one of the core problems in logistics and one of the most challenging *optimization* problems out there.

U

Unfolding / unrolling: in *recurrent neural networks*, the process of depicting the network's architecture in such a way that all the time steps are visible, enabling betting understanding of its functionality. This is done by expanding the folded *connections* in the *hidden layer* part of the network, giving it a linear form.

Unsupervised learning: a set of *data science methodologies* where there is no *target variable* that needs to be predicted.

V

Variable: a column in a dataset, be it in a matrix or a dataframe. Variables are usually turned into features, after some data engineering is performed on them.

Virtual Machine (VM): a collection of computing, storage resources, and software, taking the form of a computer, accessible via the Internet. VMs usually live in the *cloud* though there is software enabling you to create a VM on your own computer or *computer cluster*. Cloud-based VMs are very useful for AI applications.

W

Weak AI: also known as *narrow AI*, weak AI refers to a non-sentient computer system that operates within a predetermined range of skills and usually focuses on a singular task or small set of tasks. All AI in use today is weak AI.

Workflow: see *pipeline*.

APPENDIX A

Transfer Learning

It is not unusual for a complex deep learning model to train days or weeks even on today's most performant hardwares. Hence it is unpractical for many of the practitioners to re-train those useful models in order to make use of their outputs in other related tasks. Instead, using the outputs or knowledge of pre-trained models without re-training them would be more practical approach.

Transfer learning is a machine learning method that addresses this issue. More formally, transfer learning is:

> *the improvement of learning in a new task through the transfer of knowledge from a related task that has already been learned.*[37]

In simpler terms, using the outputs of a pre-trained model as inputs to another model to solve a different but somehow related task is known as transfer learning. Although, it is not specific to deep learning models, the long training times of these models make transfer learning a beneficial method for certain tasks.

---

[37] Chapter 11, Transfer Learning: https://amzn.to/2LlIxyB.

When is transfer learning useful?

In order to get most benefit out of a transfer learning application, the features learned from the first task should be general enough so that they are suitable for the second task and not specific to the first task.

When to use transfer learning

Using transfer learning should yield some measurable benefits for the second task. In general terms, the main objective of applying a transfer learning method is to decrease the training time of the second model and/or to increase the performance of it. In Figure 28, Lisa Torrey and Jude Shavlik explain the three potential benefits to search for after applying a transfer learning method.[38]

- **Higher start**: The initial skill (before refining the model) on the source model is higher than it otherwise would be.
- **Higher slope**: The rate of improvement of skill during training of the source model is steeper than it otherwise would be.
- **Higher asymptote**: The converged skill of the trained model is better than it otherwise would be.

That being said, applicability of transfer learning is usually a trial and error process as it might be hard to guess whether the approach will yield any benefits or not. However, any domain knowledge and expertise on the original task would be useful guides on when to use transfer learning.

---

[38] See the reference in the footnote 1.

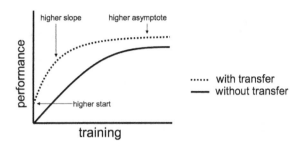

Figure 28: The three potential benefits of transfer learning. source: Chapter 11 of Handbook Of Research On Machine Learning Applications and Trends: Algorithms, Methods and Techniques.

How to apply transfer learning

We can classify the way transfer learning methods are applied into two. In the first one, the first model should be implemented and trained prior to the second one. This approach is known as "Develop Model Approach". In the second one, a pre-trained model is used without any training and its outputs are fed into the second model. This approach is known as "Pre-trained Model Approach".

Develop model approach

1. **Select a Source Task**: You first need to select a problem with an abundance of data. The relevance of features learned from this data is key to the success of the second model.

2. **Develop Your Own Source Model**: Next, you must develop your own model for this first task. The model should learn some useful features from the data. In this respect, the model selection is quite important and requires some research or prior experience.

3. **Reuse the Source Model**: The model fit on the source task will be used as a starting point for the second model to address the second task. Using this trained model should improve the performance of the second model. Depending on the nature of the problems at hand, one may directly use the output of the first model or output of one of its hidden layers as input to the second model.

4. **Tune Model**: The model may be tuned for better performance if needed.

Pre-trained model approach

1. **Select a Source Model**: Select a pre-trained model. Although there are many available pre-trained models trained on useful datasets, the features learned by this model should be relevant for the second task.

2. **Use a Pre-trained Model**: The pre-trained model will be used as a starting point for the second model to address the second task. This pre-trained model should improve the performance of the second model. Depending on the nature of the problems at hand, one may directly use the output of the pre-trained model or output of one of its hidden layers as input to the second model.

3. **Tune Model**: The model may be tuned for better performance if needed.

Applications of transfer learning

Transfer learning has many application areas in both general machine learning and deep learning. We touch here just two common application areas of it in computer vision and natural language processing.

In image recognition tasks, many research institutions develop performant models and make them public for reuse. Training these models usually takes days or even weeks. Hence, many people prefer to use these pre-trained models instead and apply a pre-trained model approach to transfer learning as explained earlier. Some examples of these models include:

- Oxford VGG Model
- Google Inception Model
- Microsoft ResNet Model

In natural language processing, it is very common to use word embeddings as input to the models. Word embeddings are vector representations of words that are trained on very large corpus data (you can think of them as meta-features similar to those resulting from PCA, but which are all useful for capturing the importance of various terms such as words or phrases, in various texts, for various NLP-related models). The words that have similar meanings are represented as vectors that are closer to each other. Two very common word embeddings are:

- Google's word2vec
- Stanford's GloVe

Many deep learning frameworks are already bundled with some of the state-of-the-art models so that you can use these pre-trained models as part of your transfer learning method. Keras also has a large set of pre-trained models integrated in it. You can use these pre-trained models by just importing Keras' applications module. You can read the documentation here[39] to learn more about Keras' applications module.

---

[39] https://keras.io/applications/.

Reinforcement Learning

We briefly cover Reinforcement Learning[40] (RL), which has applicability in a wide range of areas like game playing and finance. Resting upon a basic observation on how humans learn from their experiences, RL is one of the most important learning paradigms in machine learning and to some extent, to AI too.

Let's first look at how a baby learns whether fire is a good thing or a bad thing. Since fire illuminates the environment, baby learns that fire is something that is shining and colorful. When she gets closer to the fire, she gets warm and in cold nights that is also something very beneficial. Eventually, when she tries to touch the fire, she realizes that fire burns which is a very bad thing for a baby. Hence, from these experiments the baby learns that sometimes fire is good and sometimes it is bad. As long as she keeps the distance at some level, she can enjoy the fire.

Similar to the way of learning in our example, RL is a learning paradigm in machine learning where learning from experiments is the key tenet. More formally, RL is a type of machine learning where agents learn how to behave in

---

[40] You may also have heard of "Deep Reinforcement Learning". It is a special kind of Reinforcement Learning where the deep neural networks are used in the modeling. In this appendix, we just use Reinforcement Learning to emphasize its general applicability to many kinds of machine learning methods.

environments by observing the outcomes of their actions. In a sense, RL can be thought of a special form of trial and error in machine learning.

Applications of RL are especially popular in game playing. Also, understanding the terminology of RL in a game context is quite easy. Because of this, in the following discussion we'll give our examples from an old but still popular game: Super Mario!

Key terms

In order to speak about RL, the following four key terms should be understood:

- **Agent:** It is something that takes actions in an environment and gets the rewards. You can think of an agent as Super Mario himself in the game. RL aims at making agents learn from their environments and achieve good performances on the tasks they are given.

- **Environment:** It is the set of states that the agent operates in. You can think of it as the levels and all the objects inside that level in the Super Mario game. Environment is the data that the agents learn from.

- **Action:** It is an operation of an agent given a state of the environment. The results of actions yield rewards. An example is jumping in the Super Mario game. After each action, agents increase or decrease their total rewards. By considering the result of an action, agents learn whether an action should be taken or not, given the state.

- **Reward:** It is the benefit or punishment that the agent gets upon taking an action. You can think of it as the number of gold coins that are collected in a level or the successful finishing of a level in Super Mario.

> The objective of a RL model is to maximize the total rewards by discovering the best actions depending on the state of the environment.

Let's summarize what we've learned from the definitions of these four terms. In RL, our task is to make our agents learn the best set of actions from the environments they are given by experimenting. The term "best" means that the agent should maximize its total rewards and hence the best set of actions should result in the maximum possible total rewards. More formally, the goal of the agent is to maximize its expected cumulative rewards.

Reward hypothesis

The central optimization idea in RL rests upon the "Reward Hypothesis". According to this idea, tasks can be represented as the maximum expected cumulative rewards so that the analytical RL methods can be applied. Even if not all tasks fall into this category, there are many important tasks that fall within. If we can represent a problem along the lines of this reward hypothesis, then RL techniques can be applied to it.

Mathematically, the cumulative reward function is the sum of the rewards that agent gets after each action:

$$G(t) = R(t+1) + R(t+2) + \ldots + R(t+n)$$

In some cases however, near future should be given more weight than the distant future. To be able to do that, the rewards are multiplied by a preference parameter or a discount factor which lies between 0 and 1. By doing this, we make our agents care more about the near future than the distant future.[41]

Types of tasks

A task is an instance of a RL problem. The formula above includes "n" rewards. However, some tasks continue forever. In that respect, we have two types of tasks:

1. **Episodic Tasks:** These tasks have some ending point. So, these are tasks that are limited in terms of the number of actions and the states of the environment. In the Super Mario game, a level corresponds to an episode.

2. **Continuous Tasks:** These are the tasks that have no ending points. Hence, these tasks continue forever. For this kind of task, the reward formula we gave above should be adjusted such that the number of reward terms in the summation goes to infinity. A good example of these tasks is stock trading in finance.

RL includes many mathematical, statistical and algorithmic techniques which are beyond the scope of this book. Here we just highlighted some basic concepts of RL and its central tenets. If you are interested in RL, we encourage you to read more about it. There are many books, papers, and blog posts about RL as well as an interesting YouTube channel. The latter is called "Code Bullet" and it features several popular games (and some not-so-popular ones too), with AIs playing them, after being exposed to them through a RL process. Before closing this appendix, let's mention briefly some useful RL frameworks.

---

[41] You can also find similar functions in economics. The consumption behavior of households is usually modeled in a similar fashion in economic models.

Reinforcement learning frameworks

There are some useful frameworks that you can use if you want to dig into the RL applications. Here, we just name two of them:

1. **OpenAI Gym:** Gym is a project of OpenAI (a project created by Elon Musk to foster AI research in a democratic manner). It is a toolkit for developing and comparing RL algorithms. You can find many environments for many kind of games. Examples include cart-pole, mountain-car, Atari games, Doom, etc. You can also compare your performances against benchmarks. As of this writing Gym only supports Python.

2. **RL-Glue:** It is a project that is initiated by Professor Sutton's team in UoFA and extended by a large community. It supports languages Java, C/C++, Python, MATLAB, and Lisp. As of this writing there are more than ten tasks included in RL-Glue.

Autoencoder Systems

Autoencoder systems are a special kind of Deep Learning network that opts to perform a summarization of the original data, into a lower-dimensionality feature space. In essence, they are like PCA, ICA, and other statistical processes for creating a more compact feature set, but with one key difference: autoencoders provide a mapping that is highly non-linear and therefore able to capture all those non-linear aspects of the data. This results in a better and more robust representation (aka embedding), something particularly useful when it comes to highly complex datasets - all that while keeping the resource requirements to a manageable level.

Components

The architecture of an autoencoder is very similar to that of other DL systems, comprising a series of layers of neurons. However, autoencoders have the same number of neurons in the output layer, which corresponds to the features of the data, just like the input layer. The innermost layer (one of the hidden layers of the network) contains the optimal embedding of these features and it always has fewer neurons than the input layer. You can view a minimalistic autoencoder system in Figure 29.

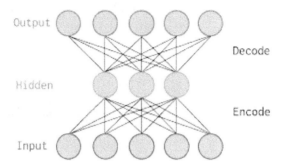

Figure 29. Graphical representation of an autoencoder network. Image created by Muhammad Abu Hijleh and available under CC license. Normally autoencoders have multiple hidden layers, just like all DL systems. The one shown here has a single one, which is also the embedding of the data.

Data flow and functionality

The data in an autoencoder initially flows from the input to the output, through all the hidden layers in-between. Once it reaches the end of the network, the outputs are compared to the original feature values as the latter take the role of the targets. The inevitable differences (errors) travel backwards and are used to modify the weights of the connections among the neurons and the whole process is repeated until the errors are below a predefined limit.

Moreover, the process of turning the input data into embedding is called encoding (or convolution), while the reverse process, whereby the data in the embedding process is turned into an approximation of the original features, in the output layer, is called decoding (or deconvolution). Finally, the data corresponding to the hidden layer is usually referred to as latent variables.

Error function

The *error function* of an autoencoder is usually the squared error between the inputs and the outputs, though depending on the problem at hand it can involve different kinds of norms of the aforementioned differences. Just like multi-level perceptrons, once computed, the error is propagated to the different parts of the network.

Extensions of conventional autoencoder models

Denoising autoencoder

This is a special kind of autoencoder, first explored in 2008 by Vincent et al. It basically works with corrupt data as its inputs and attempts to reconstruct the noisy signal. It manages that by abstracting what is called the manifold of the data, which is the shape we wish to capture when the dimensionality of the data is reduced. Once a form of the manifold is abstracted based on the input data, the autoencoder rebuilds that signal and outputs what it believes to be a more accurate representation of the original inputs.

Note that the manifold approach is common among conventional autoencoders too, since without an abstraction of the signal at hand, it would not be possible to express it in a different form, particularly a more information-rich one.

Just like in regression systems, a regularization parameter is introduced to ensure a simple and therefore more robust model. This is accomplished by introducing a parameter β corresponding to the how much weight we put on a sparser (simpler) coding: $E_s = E + \beta \cdot$Penalty.

Such a system would be also somewhat easier to interpret, while also more resistant to instability. Also, despite the seemingly convoluted processes related to sparsity and how it applies to a more robust representation, in practice it is quite straightforward, as it is quite easy to implement through the various DL frameworks.

Variational autoencoder

Variational AutoEncoders (or VAE for short) are specialized autoencoder systems that are designed for calculating the parameters of a statistical model that describes the distribution of the input data. VAEs are like conventional autoencoders but with a twist in the latent variables they generate. The idea is to create such latent variables that approximately follow a unit Gaussian distribution, instead of being arbitrary. After this is done, it's just a matter of generating new points following that distribution and passing them as inputs to the decoding part of the VAE network. For better performance, we can apply a trick of sorts, involving a process called KL divergence, which needs to be optimized.

VAEs not only produce new data that closely resembles the original dataset, but they also create data that is free of noise and also looks more realistic. This is the main reason why they are better at this task compared to Generative Adversarial Networks (GANs).

Use cases and applications

Autoencoders have a variety of use cases where they can add value. The main ones are the following:

- **Dimensionality reduction**: although PCA and t-SNE are great at this, autoencoders are a more robust and more versatile alternative that can scale up really well. T-SNE, for example cannot handle a very large number of features, while PCA requires a great deal of resources to accomplish that. Autoencoders, on the other hand, can provide a reduced feature set without any such limitations.

- **Data denoising**: various datasets, such as those comprising of multi-media data, have a lot to benefit from a denoising autoencoder.

- **Data generation**: using the specialized kind of autoencoder (VAE), we can create new data in cases where additional data is required (e.g. for training other AI models).

Generative Adversarial Networks

Generative Adversarial Networks (GANs) are a special kind of deep learning system that deserves closer attention. The main idea of a GAN is to have two competing DL networks, one specialized in learning (aka the discriminative model) and one specialized in generating cases that cannot be identified correctly by the learner (aka the generative model). The input for these new cases is plain noise. This way, with minimal data resources, it is possible to obtain a trained DL system that has a good enough generalization, even if you don't have a lot of data for its training.

Components

The architecture of a GAN is fairly straightforward, once you understand its general premise. A comprehensive view of it can be found in Figure 30. Note that the discriminator network D(x) can be any kind of DL network that can be employed in prediction analytics.

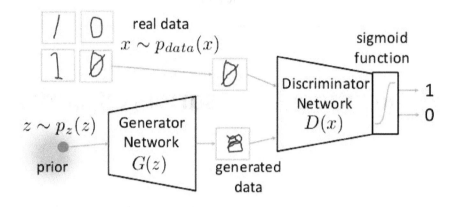

Figure 30. High-level representation of a GAN. In this representation, $P_{data}(x)$ is the distribution of the real data, while X is a sample from that distribution. $P(z)$ on the other hand is the distribution of generator, and Z is a sample from that distribution. Also, $G(z)$ and $D(x)$ represent the two DL networks comprising the GAN. Image originally published in the Analyticsvidhya blog (www.analyticsvidhya.com).

Data flow and functionality

The data in a GAN flows towards the discriminator network, which is then asked to decide whether it is of a particular class (usually 0 and 1). If the data is coming from the real dataset, the chances of it passing is log(D(x)), which corresponds to an entropy $E_1[\log(D(x)]$. Naturally, this DL system tries to maximize this quantity by making it as close to 1 as possible. On the other hand, there is a chance that the data is coming from the artificial dataset that the generative network is putting together. In this case the chance of it passing is 1 - D(G(z)), with the corresponding entropy being $E_2[\log(1 - D(G(z)))]$. Naturally, the discriminator network tries to minimize that by making it close to 0. So, overall, the objective it is pursuing (through its training) is to maximize the quantity V(D, G) = E_1 + E_2.

On the other hand, the generative network is trying to minimize the same quantity V(D, G), since this is how it can make its counterpart more accurate in its predictions. This whole process can be summarized in the following expression:

$$\min_{G} \max_{D} V(D, G)$$

Training process

When training a GAN, for a problem you have defined and collected data for, you need to apply the following process:

1. **Define the GANs architecture**. This involves the type of DL network that you are going to use for your generator and discriminator systems. Naturally, this will be a function of the data at hand.

2. **Train the discriminator system on real data for a while**. The precise number of epochs you train it for is up to you, but you definitely don't want to over-train it, since this would result in overfitting.

3. **Create a number of fake data points for the generative system to use.** Now it's the other GAN component's turn to get some data. Naturally, the outputs it yields based on that data is not very useful at first, but it needs to start somewhere.

4. **Train discriminator on the fake data resulting from the previous step**. Once the fake data is ready, feed it to the discriminator network and observe how it distinguishes it from the real data.

5. **Train generator network with the output of the previous step**. Now you do the same but for the generator system, so that it refines the fake data it produces, to make it more challenging for its counterpart to spot.

6. **Repeat steps 2 to 5 for a number of epochs.**

7. **Check fake data yourself to see if it appears similar enough to the real data.** If it does, you can stop the training, otherwise, you can repeat steps 2 to 5 for a while longer.

8. **Evaluate the performance of the discriminator system.**

Pain points of a GAN model

The main pain points of a GAN model revolve around the fact that more often than not, they are used with images. Like every other DL system, GAN models view these images as a set of numbers, making it impossible for them to truly have any real context related to the subjects of these images or what they are expected to be like.

Issues related to counting

Counting issues relate to this as the GANs often fail to comprehend that certain aspects of a subject correspond to how many of that subject exist in an image. This results in fake data often looking like some genetic experiment gone wrong, with images of creatures having multiple sets of eyes or heads.

Perspective issues

Since perspective is something that only relatively recently has been understood by our species when it comes to visual representations of the world (one of the innovations of Leonardo Da Vinci), it is no surprise that GANs often fail to deliver images that exhibit this characteristic. After all, GANs tend to view an image as a flat surface having various colors on it, much like an ancient painting.

Issues with global structures

The structures corresponding to various subjects are something we take for granted since we are used to seeing them a certain way. These structures have to do with how a subject is positioned and in the case of an animal, with its anatomy. However, GANs lack this understanding of the subjects they encounter in the images, so they come up with fake images that are very much like an amateur photo gag.

Use cases and applications

Generative Adversarial Networks have a variety of use cases, where they can add value. The main ones are the following:

- **Text to Image Generation**: This is particularly useful when you want to obtain copyright-free images using a database or a web archive as a source. The GAN translates the text into specific characteristics for the image to have, identifies images having these characteristics, and generates new images resembling the latter.

- **Image Caption Generation**: This involves finding particular characteristics of a given image, figuring out what words correspond to them (using some caption database), and creating new text that resembles the latter. Naturally, the descriptions of the images in the database need to be quite accurate.

- **Increasing Resolution of an image**: Just like denoising autoencoders, GANs can be used for cleaning up an image, though their approach is different. What they do is create new images that resemble the original one as much as possible, but with fewer similarities among neighboring pixels.

- **Predicting the next frame in a video**: Useful for spotting anomalies in the frames of a video, this application involves finding the next frame based on the image of the last frame in a video clip. This is done by creating new frames that closely resemble the previous ones, in a time-series fashion.

- **Interactive Image Generation**: This entails creating images that have certain characteristics, depicted graphically by the user in the form of rudimentary images. The GAN involved creates images using these characteristics, that are also similar to the ones it has been trained on.

- **Image to Image Translation**: This is the previous application taken to the next level. It involves using an image as input data for the generative network and allowing the GAN to learn based off that, generating similar images in the process that are also more realistic.

The Business Aspect of AI in Data Science Projects

Since data science has a strong business component to it, it is essential to examine this aspect of the craft and how AI fits into all this. After all, AI is still a fairly expensive technology if it is implemented properly, so it is far from being a panacea, when it comes to data science projects.

Factors like the relevant technologies that make AI feasible and practical, as well as the computing and data resources required, need to be taken into account when deciding whether to invest in an AI system for a data science project or not. Also, not all industries benefit from AI the same way, so this is an important consideration to have. Finally, the education a data scientist needs in order to handle AI-related projects is another factor that needs to be examined, if AI is to be a fruitful part of an organization's data science endeavors.

Description of relevant technologies

As mentioned briefly in the main text of this book, there are several technologies that go hand-in-hand with AI. A business person needs to have them in mind as how they evolve is bound to affect significantly the whole AI field. Also, investing in these technologies, particularly in terms of infrastructure, would be a sound strategic decision, if you plan to embrace AI in your organization.

The key technology in AI at the moment is GPUs. Although these are fairly commonplace, not many computers have enough GPU power to render a high-level DL system a viable option. Oftentimes specialized computers need to be built, having several GPUs accessible to them, in order to scale up their computational power so that they can implement large DL networks. The key advantage of this option is that the cost is fixed and once you create such a system, the only running cost for it is the electricity it consumes, which is negligible compared to the potential benefit it can offer (assuming you have the data to feed such an AI system).

An alternative technology to GPUs that is also very popular, is cloud computing. This involves leasing computing power, RAM, and storage space in a remote data center. The latter is a collection of specialized servers for this sort of task, usually owned and managed by a big tech company, such as Amazon or Microsoft. The cloud computing option enables you to build a virtual machine (VM) that has resources from various powerful computers, bringing about the equivalent of a supercomputer, accessible through the internet. Such a computer can handle all kinds of AI systems and is easy to scale. The key advantage of this is that you can always change its specs and customize the corresponding cost to fit your budget, at any given time period.

Another somewhat relevant technology, which is a bit experimental at this point, is *quantum computing*. Although the current AI systems don't need a quantum computer, it is quite likely that a machine like that can greatly speed up an AI system, as it would enable it to scale up to unimaginable levels, while also keeping the running cost low. Naturally, quantum computers are fairly scarce, however it is not unfathomable having the option of a shared quantum computer in the near future (much like a shared data center via a cloud). Such a technology is bound to be expensive but it might have advantages to compensate for its cost. However, everything related to this technology is still highly speculative and therefore risky, from an investment standpoint. Still, the economics of this tech may change as more players get into this industry, driving down the production cost of a quantum computer.

AI resources

Resources are important in every project. When it comes to AI-based data science, the ones that are most relevant are computing and data resources, though there is also the expertise in the specialized professionals handling these systems. The latter are covered in the final section of this appendix.

Computing resources

The computing resources of an AI-based project depend on the project's scale. They involve a lot of memory though the main bottleneck is usually the computing power, which is generally covered through a lot of GPUs. When scaling up a system, it's best to do that gradually though, since sometimes the trade-off between computing resources and time required by an AI system (mainly for its training, when it comes to deep learning systems) is manageable. Cloud computing systems are a great way to experiment with this trade-off, though for more long-term projects, it makes more sense to have your own computing infrastructure, in the form of a private cloud, aka a computer cluster.

Data resources

Data resources are something oftentimes ignored since many people have a warped perception about AI's relationship to data. Although there are AI systems that can generate data similar to what they have been trained on such as VAEs and GANs, in order for them to provide good quality data they need to have a good generalization of the dataset they are going to expand. For this to happen though, sufficient data is required, just like any other AI project.

Data science systems (particularly machine learning ones) have evolved over the years and can handle all sorts of datasets. However, for AI systems to truly offer an edge over these systems, there needs to be a lot of data available. So, getting a number of data streams in a data science pipeline and having processes in place for maintaining them (so that the data doesn't become stale) is paramount for making an AI-based system bring about sufficient value to justify its existence and the potential training of the people who use it regularly.

Industries and applications benefiting the most from AI

Naturally, industries where a lot of data is involved are more suitable for adopting AI in their data science pipelines. That's why the financial and telecommunications sectors were the first ones to adopt data science in general. Also, industries like retail can benefit a lot from AI, as they have dynamic data that is suitable for an RNN system, for example.

What's more, if you are considering an application involving lots of text, sound or image data, such as through the ingestion of social media feeds, you can get a lot out of an AI system, particularly if you have a lot of data like that. If all your data is binary and continuous variables though, you may get by with a conventional data science system too. Make sure you consult a data scientist with AI know-how when making this decision.

Data science education for AI-related projects

The use of AI in data science brings about to the forefront the data-driven paradigm. Before that, data was tackled primarily using statistical models which carried with them a set of assumptions that were not always valid. The data-driven approach doesn't have any such assumptions, making it more accurate and generally more effective, particularly when dealing with complex datasets, not following any particular distribution.

This approach to data, powered by machine learning and AI know-how, creates a new kind of role in data analytics, one that is geared more towards state-of-the-art systems. Statistics is still a useful skill to have, but it's not as important since it is useful mainly for the data exploration stage. All the heavy work in the data-driven paradigm is undertaken by specialized data models (usually AI ones) that require a different set of skills. However, this is not too different to the standard skill-set of a data scientist, so an AI specialist is not always the best option. Sometimes it is better to train existing employees on these new systems.

All this renders continuous education a necessity, so training courses and conferences ought to be included in the data science budget. Besides, most of the AI frameworks out there are free, so training someone to use them is usually a worthwhile investment.

Using Docker Image of the Book's Code and Data

Docker is a system that enables the reliable transference of programming systems to other computers. It basically ports the whole environment of a project, along with any packages that need to be installed, so that the code of the project can run smoothly. Data files can be included too, making the running of a project possible in completely different machines than the one(s) it was developed on. This way, the risk of running into errors is minimal.

A Docker image is not the same as a virtual machine, since the latter is more of a portable computer with its own operating system, resources, and storage space. Docker images are fairly lightweight and more flexible overall.

Downloading the Docker software

Before making use of the Docker image, you'll need to download and install the Docker software to your computer. Docker supports all the major operating systems like Windows, Mac or Linux. Depending on the operating system you are using, you can find the corresponding files here: https://dockr.ly/2NjJI1Q.

Note that there is also the "Docker-compose" program, which if you are using Linux you'll need to install separately. These are all the things you need to download and install to your computer.

Using Docker with an image file

First, you'll need to download the image file, which is going to be in a password-protected archive. The password for it is *AI4datascience2018* and you'll need to type it in when extracting it. Afterwards, you'll need to type the following command in order to run the Docker image:

```
Docker run --name debjulia -d -p 8888:8888 -t
    AI4datascience2018/debjulia
```

That's all. You can access the files inside the Docker image by going to *0.0.0.0:8888/* on your browser where a Jupiter notebook will be already run for you.

Docker tips

Generally, you don't need an internet connection when running the Docker image, but for the updating stage (which you only need to run once), you'll need to be connected to the internet. Also, when accessing the Jupyter application, you'll need to provide the aforementioned password again. Although the port 8888 is not used by a popular program, you need to make sure that no other program runs at port 8888 before running the Docker image. Finally, make sure that you run the Docker image on a computer with at least 4 GB of RAM.

Index

www.ingramcontent.com/pod-product-compliance
Lightning Source LLC
Chambersburg PA
CBHW080630060326
40690CB00021B/4873